PHILOSOPHY ON THE GO

PHILOSOPHY ON THE GO

JOEY GREEN

RUNNING PRESS

PHILADELPHIA • LONDON

OTHER BOOKS BY JOEY GREEN

Hellbent on Insanity

The Gilligan's Island Handbook

The Get Smart Handbook

The Partridge Family Album

Polish Your Furniture with Panty Hose

Hi Bob!

Selling Out

Paint Your House with Powdered Milk

Wash Your Hair with Whipped Cream

The Bubble Wrap Book

Joey Green's Encyclopedia of Offbeat Uses for Brand-Name Products

The Zen of Oz

The Warning Label Book

Monica Speaks

The Official Slinky Book

You Know You've Reached Middle Age If . . .

The Mad Scientist Handbook

Clean Your Clothes with Cheez Whiz

The Road to Success Is Paved with Failure

Clean It! Fix It! Eat It!

Joey Green's Magic Brands

The Mad Scientist Handbook 2

Senior Moments

Jesus and Moses: The Parallel Sayings

Joey Green's Amazing Kitchen Cures

Jesus and Muhammad: The Parallel Sayings

Joey Green's Gardening Magic

How They Met

Joey Green's Incredible Country Store

Potato Radio, Dizzy Dice

Joey Green's Supermarket Spa

Weird Christmas

Contrary to Popular Belief

Marx & Lennon: The Parallel Sayings

Joey Green's Rainy Day Magic

The Jolly President

Champagne and Caviar Again?

Joey Green's Mealtime Magic

Famous Failures

Copyright © 2007 by Joey Green.
All rights reserved under the Pan-American and International Copyright Conventions
Printed in the United States

No part of this book may be used or reproduced in any manner whatsoever without written permission of
the publisher except in the case of brief quotations embodied in critical articles or reviews.

"The Shirley Partridge Philosophy" originally appeared in *The Partridge Family Album* by Joey Green.
Copyright © 1994 by Joey Green.

"Modern Philosophy" by Joey Green and Alan Corcoran.
Copyright © 2006 by Joey Green and Alan Corcoran.

*This book may not be reproduced in whole or in part, in any form or by any means, electronic or
mechanical, including photocopying, recording, or by any information storage and retrieval system now
known or hereafter invented, without written permission from the publisher.*

9   8   7   6   5   4   3   2   1
Digit on the right indicates the number of this printing
Library of Congress Control Number: 2007921302

ISBN-13: 978-0-7624-2858-8
ISBN-10: 0-7624-2858-9

Cover illustration by Blake Looslie
"Thinkers and Stinkers" illustrations by Robert L. Prince
"Overman" illustration (page 235) by Joey Green
Edited by Jennifer Kasius

This book may be ordered by mail from the publisher.
Please include $2.50 for postage and handling.
But try your bookstore first!

Running Press Book Publishers
2300 Chestnut Street
Philadelphia, PA 19103-4371

Visit us on the web!
www.runningpress.com

"A serious and good philosophical work could be written consisting entirely of jokes."

—Ludwig Wittgenstein
(1889–1951)

TABLE OF CONTENTS

INTRODUCTION

Philosophy courses traditionally focus on the history of a few white European men who spent their dreary lives pontificating out loud until they'd put everyone else to sleep. These annoyingly cerebral philosophers basically use big words that no one can understand and bring up questions that everyone has pondered at one time or another but that most people agree can never be answered and that if you keep thinking about them, you'll drive yourself insane, which many philosophers have accomplished for themselves. In other words, most philosophers are a bunch of social misfits with nothing better to do than ponder unanswerable questions like "What is reality?" "Why are we here?" and "If I got lousy service, do I really have to leave a tip?"

To most people, philosophy seems incomprehensible. That's because most of the classic philosophers take simple ideas and express them in convoluted language peppered with esoteric phrases, obscuring what they're really trying to say.

In truth, philosophy is incredibly easy to understand. In fact, you've been practicing philosophy for years without even knowing it. Basically, philosophy is just an attempt to find answers to all those pesky questions that you think about when you're lying in bed trying to fall asleep at night. Questions like: "Why are we here?" "How did we get here?" "Who created the world?" "Is there a God, and if so, who created God?" "Where does the universe end?" "What is infinity? "Is there an afterlife, and if so, will I be able to get a good cup of coffee when I get there?" "What is the soul?" "How can I know for sure that this is reality?" "What if I'm really dreaming all this?" "What if I wake up to discover I've been in a coma for the last seventeen years?" "How many licks does it really take to get to the center of a Tootsie Pop?" "And where did I park the car?"

Professional philosophers merely continue asking questions, determined to find an answer. Unfortunately, the answers merely raise more questions that escalate way out of control, explaining why so many philosophers have flipped their lids, lost their marbles, and tossed their cookies.

So how does philosophy work exactly? Well, there are basically two ways to learn philosophy. You can study the history of philosophy and try to figure out what every major white European philosopher of the past was trying to say in his seemingly impenetrable writings. Or you can just jump in and try to figure out the answers to the questions that have haunted human beings ever since we crawled out of the primordial ooze, looked up to the stars, and said, "Hey, where did I leave my eyeglasses?" Philosophy also teaches some incredibly tedious methods used to formulate questions, answer them, and then prove yourself wrong. It's called logic, and it's really difficult to fathom because there's really no logic in how logic is taught, if you can follow that logic.

The best way for you to learn philosophy is to tackle all of these things at one time, in short easy lessons while you're sitting in the one room where you can get some quality time alone to contemplate the mysteries of the universe, like "Who used up all the toilet paper?"

In this book, I've simplified the study of philosophy so you can learn it without having to give it much thought. That may sound like a paradox, but paradoxes, as we shall see, are what philosophy is all about.

So by reading this book, you will learn enough about philosophy to confuse even the greatest philosopher in the world, fake your way through the most erudite wine–and–cheese soirée, and baffle all the guys down at Hooters. You will truly possess a deeper understanding of why philosophy is simultaneously fascinating yet tiresome, hilariously absurd yet deadly serious, overly complicated yet simple enough to learn while sitting on the can. Because, after all, that's where most philosophy belongs.

WHAT IS PHILOSOPHY?

"Rightly defined, philosophy is simply the love of wisdom."

—Marcus Tullius Cicero

"To ridicule philosophy is really to philosophize."

—Blaise Pascal

"There is only one thing a philosopher can be relied on to do, and that is to contradict other philosophers."

—William James

"Philosophy when superficially studied, excites doubt, when thoroughly explored, it dispels it."

—Francis Bacon

"Life is a gift of the immortal Gods, but living well is the gift of philosophy."

—Lucius Annaeus Seneca

"When he who hears doesn't know what he who speaks means, and when he who speaks doesn't know what he himself means—that is philosophy."

—Voltaire

"All philosophy lies in two words, 'sustain' and 'abstain.'"

—Epictetus

"Science is what you know, philosophy is what you don't know."

—Bertrand Russell

"Any religion or philosophy which is not based on a respect for life is not a true religion or philosophy."

—Albert Schweitzer

"Philosophy: unintelligible answers to insoluble problems."

—Henry Adams

"There is only one truly philosophical problem, and that is suicide."

—Albert Camus

"Sixty minutes of thinking of any kind is bound to lead to confusion and unhappiness."

—James Thurber

"The point of philosophy is to start with something so simple as not to seem worth stating, and to end with something so paradoxical that no one will believe it."

—Bertrand Russell

"History is philosophy teaching by examples."

—Dionysius

"Philosophy is an act of living."

—Plutarch

"The philosophy of one century is the common sense of the next."

—Henry Ward Beecher

"It is a great advantage for a system of philosophy to be substantially true."

—George Santayana

"The discovery of what is true and the practice of that which is good are the two most important aims of philosophy."

—Voltaire

"I am so stupid that I cannot understand philosophy; the antithesis of this is that philosophy is so clever that it cannot comprehend my stupidity. These antitheses are mediated in a higher unity: in our common stupidity."

—Søren Kierkegaard

"Leisure is the Mother of Philosophy."

—Thomas Hobbes

"The first step toward philosophy is incredulity."

—Denis Diderot

"My advice to you is not to inquire why or whither, but just enjoy your ice cream while it's on your plate—that's my philosophy."

—Thornton Wilder

"If Aristotle were alive today he'd have a talk show."

—Timothy Leary

Choose one phrase from each box, string them all together, and—*voilà*—no one will know what the hell you're talking about.

"Reality is nothing more than...

an ontological	duality	organized into
an empirical	rationalism	independent of
an atomistic	pantheism	reliant upon
a utilitarian	justification	that transcends
a pragmatic	oneness	predetermined by
a peripatetic	phenomenology	free to create

subjective	nothingness.
a metaphysical	imperative.
a transient	Gnosticism.
an omniscient	hierarchy.
existential	syllogism.
isomorphic	materialism.

God can be seen as . . .

the cause of everything		universe.
the unknowable Absolute	in the	mind of men.
the Unmoved Mover		realm of ideas.
Pure Consciousness		ultimate reality.
self-determined Oneness		one Oneness.

Hence, man is . . .	an insignificant	union of body and soul."
	a triumphant	mix of mind and matter."
	a microcosmic	waste of divine substance."
	a pathetic	evolutionary mishap."

17

THAT DARN SOCRATES

- The ancient Greek philosopher Socrates (469–399 BCE) was the antithesis of the Greek notion of beauty. Written descriptions and sculptures of Socrates that have survived to this day portray him as pug–nosed with bulging eyes, thick lips, and long, unkempt hair. He embraced poverty, rarely washed or changed his clothes, and went around barefoot.

- Socrates adamantly denied that he was a teacher, and he never accepted any money for raising questions before eager throngs of youth in the market place.

- Socrates educated others by engaging a student in conversation and questioning him innocently and almost incessantly until the student exposed a contradiction in his position and realized his own ignorance. Law school professors adopted this "Socratic method" of continuously questioning an individual student in front of the entire class to push the student to defend a position, think on his feet, and learn how to raise questions on his own.

- No writings exist from Socrates. Everything we know about him comes from the writings of his contemporaries Plato, Aristophanes, and Xenophon.

- Socrates was married and had three children.

- In his play *The Clouds,* the ancient Greek comic playwright Aristophanes caricatured Socrates, suspending him in a basket over his disciples' heads and depicting him as a bumbling fool with far–fetched theories.

- Socrates was more than seventy years old when the Athenian assembly convicted him of impiety and corrupting youth and a jury of two thousand people condemned him to death. Socrates refused to renounce what he believed to be right, choosing instead to be condemned to death by the law. He also refused to escape when he had the chance to do so.

- The painting "The Death of Socrates" by French artist Jacques-Louis David depicts a resolute and noble Socrates, unjustly condemned to death yet steadfastly committed to his ideals, about to drink the hemlock that killed him. Thomas Jefferson was present at the unveiling of the painting in 1787.

Socrates Condensed ➡◀

Convinced that the highest form of human excellence is to question oneself and others, Socrates believed that the highest good is knowledge, which enables the individual to choose the morally and ethically correct course of action. Like whether an unexamined life is worth living.

WHAT SOCRATES SAID

"Know thyself."

"A life unexamined is not worth living."

"I know that I am intelligent, because I know that I know nothing."

"Employ your time in improving yourself by other men's writings, so that you shall gain easily what others have labored hard for."

"Children today are tyrants. They contradict their parents, gobble their food, and tyrannize their teachers."

"Bad men live to eat and drink, whereas good men eat and drink in order to live."

"Think not those faithful who praise all your words and actions, but those who kindly reprove your faults."

"What you cannot enforce, do not command."

"Let a man be of good cheer about his soul. When the soul has been arrayed in her own proper jewels—temperance and justice, and courage, and nobility and truth—she is ready to go on her journey when the hour comes."

"By all means marry; if you get a good wife you'll become happy; if you get a bad one you'll become a philosopher."

"In every one of us there are two ruling and directing principles, whose guidance we follow wherever they may lead; the one being an innate desire of pleasure; the other, an acquired judgment which aspires after excellence."

"If a rich man is proud of his wealth, he should not be praised until it is known how he uses it."

"He is not only idle who does nothing, but he is idle who might be better employed."

"He is richest who is content with the least, for content is the wealth of nature."

"Beauty is a short–lived tyranny."

"Only the extremely ignorant or the extremely intelligent can resist change."

"He who is not contented with what he has, would not be contented with what he would like to have."

"Contentment is natural wealth, luxury is artificial poverty."

"My belief is that to have no wants is divine."

"I thought to myself, 'I am wiser than this man: neither of us knows anything that is really worthwhile, but he thinks he has knowledge when he has not, while I, having no knowledge, do not think that I have. I seem, at any rate, to be a little wiser than he is on this point: I do not think that I know what I do not know.'"

"Let him that would move the world, first move himself."

"The only true knowledge consists in knowing that we know nothing."

"The way to gain a good reputation is to endeavor to be what you desire to appear."

"False words are not only evil in themselves, but they infect the soul with evil."

FAMOUS PHILOSOPHY MAJORS

Think you'll never get a job if you major in something as esoteric as philosophy in college? Well, think again. Below you'll discover just some of the many successful people who majored in philosophy, proving that existence really does precede essence.

Steve Allen
Comedian, author, and former host of *The Tonight Show*

Woody Allen
Comedian, director, and writer

Wes Anderson
Director of the movies *Rushmore* and *The Royal Tenenbaums*

Max Baer Jr.
Actor who starred as Jethro on the television sitcom *The Beverly Hillbillies*

Kristen Baker
First female captain at West Point

William Bennett
Former United States secretary of Education and former director of the Office of National Drug Control Policy

Stephen Breyer
United States Supreme Court Justice

Jerry Brown
Former governor of California and presidential candidate

Pat Buchanan
Green party nominee in 2000 for president of the United States

Pearl S. Buck
Novelist and Nobel prize winner

George Carlin
Comedian

John Chancellor
Journalist and television news anchor

Mary Higgins Clark
Novelist and mystery writer

William Jefferson Clinton
Forty-second president of the United States

Angela Davis
Radical activist

Philip K. Dick
Science fiction writer

David Duchovny
Actor who played Fox Mulder on *The X–Files*

T.S. Eliot
Poet, dramatist, and literary critic who won the Nobel prize for literature

John Elway
Quarterback for the Denver Broncos

Phil Jackson
NBA coach and former player for the New York Knicks

Rahm Emanuel
Illinois congressman

Carly Fiorina
Former CEO of Hewlett-Packard

Ken Follett
Author of thrillers and historical novels

Harrison Ford
Actor who played Hans Solo in *Star Wars* and Indiana Jones in *Raiders of the Lost Ark*

J. Paul Getty
Industrialist, founder of the Getty Oil Company, and benefactor of the Getty Art Museum

Rudy Giuliani
Former mayor of New York City

Phillip Glass
Composer

Chris Hardwick
Actor who hosted MTV's *Singled Out*

Gary Hart
United States senator and former presidential candidate

Vaclav Havel
Playwright and former president of Czechoslovakia

Carl Icahn
American billionaire financier

Pope John Paul II
Second-longest reigning pontiff

Martin Luther King Jr.
Civil rights leader

Beverly McLachlin
First female chief justice of the Canadian Supreme Court

Jimmy Kimmel
Comedian and host of *The Jimmy Kimmel Show*

Aung San Suu Kyi
Human rights activist and Nobel Peace Prize winner

Bruce Lee
Martial artist and actor

Jay Leno
Comedian and host of *The Tonight Show*

Gerald Levine
CEO of Time Warner

Peter Lynch
Movie director

Steve Martin
Comedian and actor best known for his movies *The Jerk* and *Father of the Bride*

Michael McCaskey
Chairman of the board of the Chicago Bears Football Club

Robert McNamara
Former president of the Ford Motor Company, former Secretary of Defense, and former president of the World Bank

Dennis Miller
Comedian, former "Weekend Update" anchor on *Saturday Night Live*, and host of *The Dennis Miller Show*

Robert Motherwell
Painter

Neil Peart
Drummer for the rock group Rush

Brad Roberts
Lead singer and guitarist for the Canadian rock group The Crash Test Dummies

Stone Phillips
Lead anchor on the NBC newsmagazine show *Dateline*

Chaim Potok
Novelist

Richard Riordan
Former mayor of Los Angeles

Joan Rivers
Comedian

Susan Sarandon
Academy Award-winning actress who starred in the movies *Bull Durham, Thelma and Louise,* and *Dead Man Walking*

Mike Schmidt
Former third baseman for the Philadelphia Phillies

Eric Severeide
Former commentator on the *CBS Evening News*

Gene Siskel
Movie reviewer for the *Chicago Tribune* who, along with Roger Ebert, reviewed movies on the television show *Siskel & Ebert*

Jeff Smith
Host of the television cooking show *The Frugal Gourmet*

Alexander Solzhenitsyn
Russian novelist, historian, and political dissident

Susan Sontag
Essayist, novelist, and activist

George Soros
Financial speculator, billionaire founder of the Soros Foundation, philanthropist, and political activist

David Souter
United States Supreme Court Justice

P. Michael Spence
Economist and Nobel prize winner

Aaron Taylor
Offensive tackle for the Green Bay Packers

Dave Thomas
Comedian who played one of the "Mackenzie Brothers" on *Second City Television*

Steve Thomas
Host of the television show *This Old House*

Alex Trebek
Host of the television game show *Jeopardy!*

Pierre Trudeau
Former Canadian Prime Minister

David Foster Wallace

Novelist and MacArthur prize recipient

Joseph A. Wapner

Judge on the television show *The People's Court*

Elie Wiesel

Author, human rights activist, and winner of the Nobel Peace Prize

George F. Will

Journalist, author, and Pulitzer Prize winner

Juan Williams

Author, columnist for *The Washington Post*, and correspondent on National Public Radio

COMPLEX PHILOSOPHIC
IDEAS MADE SIMPLE

Atomism

Everything is made from atoms. Except for protons, neutrons, and electrons.

Confucianism

Everything can be summed up with a pithy sentence that fits inside a fortune cookie.

Cynicism

Philosophy, Schmilosophy.

Deism

God created the universe, lets it run according to natural law, and just sits back with a box of popcorn and watches the show.

Empiricism

All knowledge comes from experience, which means the only way to learn something is the hard way.

Epistemology
How to differentiate between fact and opinion, so you can honestly answer the question, "Do I look fat in this dress?"

Existentialism
Life is ultimately futile and absurd. You are completely free to do as you choose, but you are fully responsible for your choices. Like whether your socks match.

Gnosticism
By acquiring knowledge about the nature of the universe, the spark of the divine imprisoned in your body can be freed to reunite with God, like a moth flying into a halogen light bulb.

Hedonism
Party! Party! Party!

Humanism
Stop praying to God to solve your problems and do your damn homework yourself.

Idealism
Reality is all an idea in your mind or God's mind. So this book doesn't really exist. It's just an idea planted in your brain.

Materialism
Nothing exists except matter and motion, so all that talk about God and the human soul is a crock.

Mechanism
Everything can be explained through physics and chemistry, so pay attention in class.

Metaphysics

The attempt to figure out the ultimate nature of things that makeup the universe. As Portuguese author Fernando Pessoa put it: "Look, there's no metaphysics on earth like chocolates."

Monism

Everything in the universe is made from the same substance—and it's not processed cheese.

Neoplatonism

By living virtuously and attaining knowledge of God, the human soul can transcend the imperfect material world and reunite with God. But only on Tuesdays and Thursdays.

Pantheism

Everything in the universe is a part of God, including the punctuation mark at the end of this sentence.

Peripatetic Philosophy

The philosophy of Aristotle, named for his habit of walking with his disciples at the Lyceum as he philosophized (also known as "walking and talking at the same time").

Phenomenology

Everything we know derives from our consciousness, triggered by phenomena and hindered by our preconceived notions. In other words, just thinking about phenomenology makes your head hurt.

Philosophes
During the eighteenth-century Enlightenment, a group of French intellectuals (including Denis Diderot, Montesquieu, Jean Jacques Rousseau, and Voltaire) believed in progress through science, reason, and snippy wisecracks.

Positivism
All we really know for sure is what can be proven scientifically or mathematically, so yes, you need to learn algebra.

Pragmatism
An abstract idea is useful only if it has some practical application. So get off your lazy butt and mow the lawn already.

Rationalism
Knowledge can be attained only through reason, because our sense perception is unreliable. Think about it.

Realism
If a tree falls in the forest and there's no one there to hear it, it still makes a noise.

Skepticism
Yeah, right. Give me a break for crying out loud.

Sophist Philosophy
Laws are just customs, so if you can get away with it, you rock, girlfriend.

Stoic Philosophy

All people possess reason, enabling everyone to relate to each other and to cosmic law, making us all citizens of the world. People achieve happiness by being logical, not emotional—just like Mr. Spock and his fellow Vulcans.

Utilitarianism

An action is right if it brings happiness, and an action that brings happiness to the most people is totally awesome, dude.

PLATO VS. PLAY-DOH

- Molded by his teacher, Socrates.

- Molded by teachers and students everywhere.

- Founded the Academy, considered the first University.

- Founded the Play-Doh Fun Factory, considered the first of its kind.

- Greatly influenced the development of Aristotle.

- Greatly influenced the development of Silly Putty.

- Developed a literary form called the dialogue, a conversation between two people discussing philosophical ideas.

- Developed as a non-toxic reusable modeling compound by two people, Noah and Joseph McVicker.

- Dialogues include *The Apology, Cratylus, Crito, Euthyphro, Gorgias, The Laws, Meno, Parmenides, Phaedo, Phaedrus, Protagoras, The Republic, The Sophist, The Symposium, Theaetetus, and Timaeus.*

- Ingredients include wheat flour, water, deodorized petroleum distillate, salt, a hardening agent, a drying agent, coloring, and perfume.

- Encouraged others to think for themselves and shape unique ideas.

- Encourages children to use their imaginations and shape unique creations.

- Insisted that the shape and size of an individual thing may vary, but the common form in which it participates does not.

- A snake rolled from Play-Doh may vary in size or shape, but the common form of a snake does not.

- Claimed that Forms exist only in the mind, not in space or time.

- Taught that Forms have greater reality than objects observed by the senses.

- Believed all people desire happiness.

- Shaped notion that committing a wrong is worse than suffering a wrong.

- Said the soul is divided into three parts: intellect, will, and desire. Intellect must use will to control desire.

- Taught that everything in the world is always becoming something else, nothing stays the same.

- Believed that although the body dies, the soul is immortal.

- Taught that after death, the soul goes to the realm of pure forms and then returns to the world in another body.

- Insisted that artists cannot usually explain their own work because they create because they are seized by "divine madness."

- Had a great influence on Western Civilization, and millions of people have studied his work.

- The original formula for Play-Doh exists and remains top secret.

- Teaches that the concept of a snake rolled from Play-Doh is perfect compared with an actual snake rolled from Play-Doh.

- Playing with Play-Doh produces happiness.

- Shaped without any rules or wrong way to play.

- Originally introduced in three colors: blue, red, and yellow. Children must use will power to avoid mixing colors together.

- Teaches that everything can be shaped into something else, and Play-Doh never stays the same.

- Although Play-Doh dries up and can no longer be used, more can be bought at a toy store.

- After destroying your creation, Play-Doh is returned to the can so it can be used over and over again.

- Allows children to create imaginary worlds, and explore textures and shapes, uninhibited by rules or instructions.

- Play-Doh is sold in more than 75 countries, and more than two billion cans of Play-Doh have been sold since 1956.

THOSE DARN DIALOGUES

Although no writings exist from Socrates, his student Plato wrote numerous "Socratic dialogues," conversations between two people discussing philosophical ideas, that reveal Socrates' method of teaching his students through a relentless series of questions.

A Dialogue Concerning a Tree Falling in the Woods

SOCRATES: So tell me, Plato. If a tree falls in the woods and there is no one there to hear it, does it make a noise?

PLATO: Certainly.

SOCRATES: What makes you so sure?

PLATO: I am not certain at all.

SOCRATES: So then, when I asked you the question, why did you answer "Certainly"?

PLATO: Did I?

SOCRATES: Yes, indeed.

PLATO: Was there anyone else to witness this occurrence?

SOCRATES: The tree falling? No, there was no one to witness it.

PLATO: No, I mean, did anyone witness that I just said "Certainly"?

SOCRATES: There, you said it again.

PLATO: I did not.

SOCRATES: Did too.

PLATO: So how can you be sure that I said it?

SOCRATES: Not so fast, pipsqueak. I see what you're trying to do here.

PLATO: And what might that be?

SOCRATES: You're trying to outwit me.

PLATO: Socrates, may I ask you a question?

SOCRATES: Assuredly.

PLATO: If Socrates asks a question and there is no one there to hear it, does it require an answer?

SOCRATES: Dear friend, surely you vex me.

A Dialogue Concerning the Chicken and the Egg

SOCRATES: Plato, I should like to ask you a question.

PLATO: Now there's a surprise. What is it?

SOCRATES: So tell me, which do you think came first? The chicken or the egg?

PLATO: Is this some sort of trick question?

SOCRATES: Possibly. I can't be sure. You're the first person I've ever asked.

PLATO: Great, so I'm your guinea pig.

SOCRATES: Victim might be more accurate.

PLATO: Well, I'd have to say the egg.

SOCRATES: What about it?

PLATO: The egg came first.

SOCRATES: Why the egg?

PLATO: Because eggs hatch into chickens.

SOCRATES: All right, then where did the egg come from?

PLATO: The egg was purchased at the grocery store.

SOCRATES: Then where did the grocery store get it?

PLATO: What a ridiculous question. From a farmer, obviously.

SOCRATES: I see. And where did the farmer get it?

PLATO: From the hen house. The hens lay eggs.

SOCRATES: Well, hens are chickens, are they not?

PLATO: Technically, yes.

SOCRATES: So if the chicken lays the egg, then did the chicken not come first?

PLATO: No, because that chicken hatched from an egg.

SOCRATES: But Plato, did not that egg in turn come from a chicken?

PLATO: Yes, but last night my wife and I had dinner at the Olive Garden. I ordered a cheese omelet. She ordered the Chicken Kiev. When the waiter returned with our food, he brought the chicken first. So you see, the chicken comes before the egg.

SOCRATES: But did you not say earlier that the egg came first?

PLATO: Ooops! You're absolutely right. My mistake. The chicken definitely came first.

SOCRATES: Thank you, Plato, you have helped me immensely.

PLATO: I have? How so?

WAITER: Are you two gentlemen ready to order lunch?

SOCRATES: Yes, please. I'll have the chicken.

A Dialogue Concerning Who's on First

SOCRATES: There's a baseball game being played in Athens, and the visiting team has Who on first.

PLATO: For shame, Socrates, even you must know that baseball hasn't been invented yet.

SOCRATES: That's beside the point. Pretend that it has been invented. Who's on first.

PLATO: How can I possibly discuss something that hasn't been invented yet? I don't even know what baseball is.

SOCRATES: All right, then, forget about baseball. Who's on first.

PLATO: I don't understand. What is first?

SOCRATES: No, What's on second.

PLATO: Forgive me, Socrates, but what is second?

SOCRATES: No, Plato, you do not understand. What is *on* second.

PLATO: Second what?

SOCRATES: No, there is only one What.

PLATO: So how can there be a second?

SOCRATES: There is a first, a second, and a third.

PLATO: But you said there is only one What. Now you are saying there are three. Who's the third?

SOCRATES: No, Who's on first.

PLATO: First what?

SOCRATES: All right. What about him?

PLATO: What about who?

SOCRATES: He's on first.

PLATO: Listen, Socrates, I hate to be rude, but this conversation seems to be going around in circles, and frankly, it's giving me a headache. Can we continue this discussion tomorrow?

SOCRATES: Tomorrow? That's our shortstop.

A Dialogue Concerning the Light in the Refrigerator

SOCRATES: Ah, Plato, I have a question for you.

PLATO: Oy vey, here we go again.

SOCRATES: When you shut the refrigerator door, how do you really know if the light turns off in there?

PLATO: Socrates, surely you realize that the neither the refrigerator nor the light bulb will be invented until the nineteenth century.

SOCRATES: Picky, picky.

PLATO: Well, I hate to burst your bubble, but this is only the fourth century BC.

Socrates: Use your imagination, for Christ's sakes.

Plato: Who is Christ?

Socrates: You know how you just told me this is the fourth century BC?

Plato: Yes.

Socrates: Well, "BC" stands for "Before Christ." That's why we've been counting the years backwards. After Christ, we'll start counting the years forwards.

Plato: Are you sure "BC" doesn't stand for "Before Confucius"?

Socrates: I'm positive. Confucius died when I was ten years old.

Plato: Good point. What did he say about the light bulb in the refrigerator?

Socrates: Nothing. I never got the chance to ask him.

Plato: Pity.

Socrates: Now then, does the light bulb go off when you shut the refrigerator door?

Plato: Well, I certainly hope so, otherwise I'll be ringing up a huge electric bill.

Socrates: Excellent thinking. But is there any way to prove that it goes off?

Plato: I have an idea, Socrates. Why don't you get inside this refrigerator?

Socrates: All right.

Plato: Are you comfortable?

Socrates: Assuredly.

Plato: Now I'll just close the door.

Socrates: Fine.

Plato: Socrates, can you still hear me?

Socrates: Yes.

Plato: Did the light go off?

Socrates: Yes. It is completely dark in here. The light is most definitely off. Plato? Can you hear me? Open the door. Hello? C'mon Plato, stop kidding around. It's getting cold in here. Hello? Plato?

HOW MANY PHILOSOPHERS DOES IT TAKE TO CHANGE A LIGHT BULB?

Socrates (469–399 BCE)

"A light bulb unexamined is not worth changing."

Plato (circa 427–circa 347 BCE)

"There is no need to change the light bulb because the only true light is knowledge."

Aristotle (384–322 BCE)

"First we must understand what we mean by change."

Epicurus (circa 342–270 BCE)

"We must consider whether changing the light bulb will bring pleasure or pain before we decide whether to change it at all."

St. Augustine (354–430)

"God controls the destiny of the light bulb, and man has the free will to choose whether to change the light bulb or to live in darkness."

Thomas Aquinas (circa 1225–1274)

"Man, endowed with both intelligence and a will, uses his intelligence to determine whether the light bulb needs to be changed, and can use his will to change the light bulb if he wishes to do so."

Francis Bacon (1561–1626)

"Man can consider objectively whether the light bulb needs to be changed, but must ultimately subject himself to the will of God and change the light bulb."

Thomas Hobbes (1588–1679)

"The dead light bulb, subject to the laws of cause and effect, causes man to deliberate until he reaches the final desire to change the light bulb, an act which is predetermined."

René Descartes (1596–1650)

"The light bulb is subject to a predetermined mechanical process based on the laws of cause and effect, but man is free to choose whether or not to change it."

Benedict Spinoza (1632–1677)

"God is the light bulb, and the light bulb is God, who set everything in the universe into motion on a predetermined course, a successive chain of cause and effect in which the light bulb dies, man changes the light bulb, the light bulb dies yet again, and so on."

John Locke (1632–1704)

"Every individual has the power to decide whether he wishes to change the light bulb, and by gathering ideas about the light bulb from experience, man comes up with the notion of whether the light bulb needs changing."

Gottfried Wilhelm Leibniz (1646–1716)

"The millions of independent, self–determined monads that comprise man freely decide whether the individual's strongest desire is to change the light bulb, and if so, they collectively strive to do so."

George Berkeley (1685–1753)

"A working light bulb is an idea in God's mind and exists spiritually, not materially."

Voltaire (1694–1778)

"This is the best of all possible light bulbs."

David Hume (1711–1776)

"The existence of the light bulb cannot be proven, and therefore it does not need to be changed."

Immanuel Kant (1724–1804)

"Although it is impossible to prove the existence of the light bulb, man needs to change the light bulb in order to see clearly at night."

Johann Gottlieb Fichte (1762–1814)

"An individual ego that is part of the Absolute ego of the universe changes the light bulb."

Friedrich Ernst Daniel Schleiermacher (1768–1834)

"God and the light bulb are one, and an individual ego, bestowed with the ability to change a light bulb, must do so to help enable the Absolute to fully realize itself."

Georg Wilhelm Friedrich Hegel (1770–1831)

"Changing the light bulb allows the universe to continue unfolding and evolving, enabling God to become self–conscious."

Arthur Schopenhauer (1788–1860)

"Although the light bulb has the will to change itself, it cannot effect this change without help from the will of man, who, if he desires enlighten-ment, need not sacrifice his own self–interests to do so."

John Stuart Mill (1806–1873)

"Whether an individual will change a light bulb depends of several factors, including the desire of the individual."

Friedrich Nietzsche (1844–1900)

"The light bulb is dead."

Martin Heidegger (1889–1976)

"The phenomena of the light-bulb-as-such prompts a confrontation with nothingness in which man must first come to grips with the truth of being-itself in the totality of Being."

Jean–Paul Sartre (1905–1980)

"Man despairs over the dead light bulb and feels anxiety toward the futil-ity of changing it, but by doing so, he introduces meaning into the world and realizes himself."

THINKERS AND STINKERS

EVERYONE LOVES ARISTOTLE

- The ancient Greek philosopher Aristotle (384–322 BCE) was a student of Plato (who was in turn a student of Socrates) and became a tutor to teenage Alexander the Great, who later became king of Macedonia and conquered much of what was the civilized world.

- Like Plato, Aristotle wrote dialogues, but most of them have been lost.

- Aristotle was an orphan by the age of ten, was raised by his uncle, and at the age of eighteen, went to Athens to study under Plato at his Academy.

- When Plato died, Aristotle was thought to be next in line to run the Academy, but instead, the position went to Plato's nephew.

- Aristotle married Pythias, and the couple had a daughter named Pythias after her mother and a son, Nicomachus.

- Aristotle founded a school in Athens called the Lyceum, named for its temple to Lycian Apollo. In 1996, archeologists discovered the lost ruins of the Lyceum.

- After the death of Alexander the Great, Athens declared war against Macedonia and charged Aristotle with impiety, the same charge that had been used to condemn Socrates to death. Aristotle said, "I will not allow the Athenians to sin twice against philosophy" and fled to Chalcis, where he died of disease a year later.

- Actor Telly Savalas' real name is Aristotelis Savalas. Best known as the star of the television police drama series *Kojak*, Savalas popularized the catchphrase "Who loves ya, baby?"

- Basketball star Shaquille O'Neal is nicknamed "The Big Aristotle."

Aristotle Condensed ➡️⬅️

Aristotle believed that the goal of life is to attain happiness and that people can achieve happiness only by leading an ethical life guided by reason. In other words, Aristotle would never buy a Hummer or drive while talking on a cell phone.

WHAT ARISTOTLE SAID

"He overcomes a stout enemy who overcomes his own anger."

"Anybody can become angry—that is easy; but to be angry with the right person, and to the right degree, and at the right time, and for the right purpose, and in the right way—that is not within everybody's power and is not easy."

"The ideal man bears the accidents of life with dignity and grace, making the best of the circumstances."

"Beauty is the gift of God."

"Personal beauty is a greater recommendation than any letter of reference."

"The best political community is formed by citizens of the middle class."

"Change in all things is sweet."

"To be conscious that we are perceiving or thinking is to be conscious of our own existence."

"The beauty of the soul shines out when a man bears with composure one heavy mischance after another, not because he does not feel them, but because he is a man of high and heroic temper."

"Dissimilarity of habit tends more than anything to destroy affection."

"It is well to be up before daybreak, for such habits contribute to health, wealth, and wisdom."

"Educated men are as much superior to uneducated men as the living are to the dead."

"Education is the best provision for old age."

"We are what we repeatedly do. Excellence then, is not an act, but a habit."

"Wishing to be friends is quick work, but friendship is a slow ripening fruit."

"All who have meditated on the art of governing mankind have been convinced that the fate of empires depends on the education of youth."

"Art not only imitates nature, but also completes its deficiencies."

"At his best, man is the noblest of all animals; separated from law and justice he is the worst."

"Bashfulness is an ornament to youth, but a reproach to old age."

"Boys should abstain from all use of wine until their eighteenth year, for it is wrong to add fire to fire."

"Education is an ornament in prosperity and a refuge in adversity."

"Never discourage anyone who continually makes progress, no matter how slow."

"No great genius is without an admixture of madness."

"Plato is dear to me, but dearer still is truth."

"Pleasure in the job puts perfection in the work."

"The aim of the wise is not to secure pleasure, but to avoid pain."

"The antidote for fifty enemies is one friend."

"The worst form of inequality is to try to make unequal things equal."

"There is a foolish corner in the brain of the wisest man."

"Those who are too smart to engage in politics are punished by being governed by those who are dumber."

"All men by nature desire knowledge."

"The end of labor is to gain leisure."

"He who has never learned to obey cannot be a good commander."

"Liars when they speak the truth are not believed."

"Misfortune shows those who are not really friends."

"Patience is bitter, but its fruit is sweet."

"Poverty is the parent of revolution and crime."

"It is the mark of an educated mind to be able to entertain a thought without accepting it."

"Happiness depends upon ourselves."

"Those that know, do. Those that understand, teach."

"We give up leisure in order that we may have leisure, just as we go to war in order that we may have peace."

"Wit is educated insolence."

PHILOSOPHY'S GREATEST HITS

You can read the greatest philosophy books ever written, or you can read these brief synopses and pretend you have read any one of these classics by simply reciting the pithy remarks conveniently provided below.

The Republic
by Plato (circa 427–circa 347 BCE)

SYNOPSIS: In these cleverly written dialogues, Socrates tries, by bombarding others with a protracted sequence of pesky questions, to discover "What is the point of being good?"

PITHY REMARK: "I loved *The Republic*, but it doesn't hold a candle to Plato's *Gorgias*."

Nicomachean Ethics
by Aristotle (384–322 BCE)

SYNOPSIS: These notes from Aristotle's lectures at the Lyceum, possibly edited by his son, Nicomachus, focus on the importance of behaving ethically and developing a virtuous character.

PITHY REMARK: "You know, you can't read *Nicomachean Ethics* without following up by reading Aristotle's *Politics*. He intended them to be two parts of the same treatise."

Leviathan
by Thomas Hobbes (1588–1679)

SYNOPSIS: Portraying the state as a monstrous, unwieldy giant with a body made of citizens and the king as its head, Hobbes argues that the commonwealth requires an absolute sovereignty to maintain civic unity, provide security, and guarantee the common defense.

PITHY REMARK: "Ah yes, 'the life of man, solitary, poor, nasty, brutish, and short.' Touché, Mr. Hobbes, touché!"

Meditations on First Philosophy
by René Descartes (1596–1650)

SYNOPSIS: Abandoning of all his preconceived notions, the Meditator attempts to reconstruct the foundation of all his knowledge and, refusing to trust his senses, withdraws into his mind and reasons that only his own self-conscious awareness proves that he truly exists (and that this book would make a terrible movie).

PITHY REMARK: "Yes, but to appreciate all the nuances, you simply must read Descartes in the original French."

An Essay Concerning Human Understanding
by John Locke (1632–1704)

SYNOPSIS: In his tediously long and painstakingly detailed theory of knowledge, Locke speculates that the mind learns about the world through sense perceptions that are then interpreted and evaluated by mental processes—making this book a guaranteed cure for insomnia.

PITHY REMARK: "I find Locke rather pedestrian compared with George Berkeley. His *Treatise Concerning the Principles of Human Knowledge* is the ultimate page–turner."

Candide
by Voltaire (1694–1778)

SYNOPSIS: In this wickedly delightful satire, Candide searches for the best of all possible worlds and ends up cultivating his own garden. Leonard Bernstein wrote an operetta titled *Candide*, based on the book.

PITHY REMARK: "Frankly, I find Voltaire's caricature of Gottfried Leibniz as Dr. Pangloss rather juvenile, don't you?"

The Social Contract
by Jean–Jacques Rousseau (1712–1778)

SYNOPSIS: "Man is born free, but he is everywhere in chains," says Rousseau, who goes on to explain that people freely join a civil society, but the state then limits freedom. Instead, all citizens must agree upon a social contract, giving legitimate political authority to the state that then expresses a general will that work toward the common good.

PITHY REMARK: "*The Social Contract* would be virtually flawless if Rousseau hadn't insisted upon a state religion."

A Treatise of Human Nature
by David Hume (1711–1776)

SYNOPSIS: Attempting to base philosophy on the study of human nature, Hume insists that we cannot base our knowledge of the external world upon our sensory experience. Instead, he says, we can only examine the psychology of our beliefs about that external world.

PITHY REMARK: "After reading this book, it's obvious why it failed to attract any attention when it was first published—because, as Hume said, there are no causal connections."

Critique of Pure Reason
by Immanuel Kant (1724–1804)

SYNOPSIS: Discussing the nature and limits of human knowledge, Kant condemns man's tendency to make generalizations based on a few cases.

PITHY REMARK: "Of all the books I've read, this is the one I wish Hollywood would make into a movie."

Utilitarianism
by John Stuart Mill (1806–1873)

SYNOPSIS: Arguing that actions are right if they promote pleasure, wrong if they produce pain, Mill argues that pleasures of the intellect and virtuous living are more revered than physical pleasures.

PITHY REMARK: "John Stuart Mill would agree that if you find reading *Utilitarianism* painful, it is wrong for you to read it."

The Communist Manifesto
by Karl Marx (1818–1883) and Friedrich Engels (1820–1895)

SYNOPSIS: This handy little book inspired the rise of the Soviet Union and originated the nifty catchphrase, "From each according to his abilities, to each according to his needs."

PITHY REMARK: "I agree with Marx and Engel's call for the abolition of private property, but abolishing child labor in factories? What are they, crazy?"

Thus Spake Zarathustra
by Friedrich Nietzsche (1844–1900)

SYNOPSIS: After living alone in a cave for ten years, Zarathustra pops into town to teach everyone his concept of the Overman, the highly evolved individual who has mastered self–control over his animal passions and rechannels them through creativity, but no one seems to care except a tightrope walker. Does this mean that only the Flying Wallendas are worthy of Nietzsche's insights?

PITHY REMARK: "If we're all going to relive every moment of our life for eternity, as Zarathustra says, that means I'll be reading this book again and again and again—Oh God, kill me now."

The Problems of Philosophy
by Bertrand Russell (1872–1970)

SYNOPSIS: Knowledge obtained from experience, says Russell, is based on our interpretation of sense–data, which seems to indicate that physical matter exists. Of course, the real "problems of philosophy" are the hundreds of pages of this impenetrable blather.

PITHY REMARK: "Why don't we go back to your place for some sense–data?"

Being and Time
by Martin Heidegger (1889–1976)

SYNOPSIS: In this dense explanation of the study of Being, Heidegger attempts to explain existence, in and of itself, by answering the question, "Why is there something rather than nothing?"

PITHY REMARK: "Reading Heidegger helps me confront nothingness and gives me constant awareness of my connection with Being."

No Exit
by Jean-Paul Sartre (1905–1980)

SYNOPSIS: A man and two women find themselves locked in a room together—only to discover that they have been eternally damned and that "Hell is other people."

PITHY REMARK: "Sartre clearly seems to be commenting not on human nature but rather on his *ménage-a-trois* with Simone de Beauvoir and Olga Kosakiewicz."

The Myth of Sisyphus
by Albert Camus (1913–1960)

SYNOPSIS: In Greek mythology, Sisyphus was condemned to forever roll a giant boulder to the top of a mountain only to have it roll back down to the bottom every time he reached the top. Camus says humans, like Sisyphus, can achieve happiness only if they accept that life is an absurd struggle.

PITHY REMARK: "If life is meaningless, why does Camus insist that we find meaning in the meaninglessness of it all?"

The Myth of the Cave

In *The Republic,* Plato wrote an allegory for mankind's understanding of reality. Imagine, says Plato, an underground cave connected to the outside world by a long tunnel that doesn't allow any sunlight to enter the cave. Inside the cave, prisoners sit facing the back wall, their backs to the entrance, shackled to the floor with chains that prevent them from turning their head around to see each other or themselves. The prisoners have been in the cave their entire lives. They know nothing other than the cave. Behind them is a bright fire, which they cannot turn around to see, and between the fire and where the men sit is a wall, and people walk behind the wall carrying pottery, statues, and figures of animals that cast shadows on the back wall in front of the shackled men. The voices of the people carrying the objects echo all over the cave. The imprisoned men, having no other experiences, assume that the shadows on the wall have a life of their own, moving and making sounds.

If one of those prisoners was freed from his shackles and allowed to stand up and turn around, he would at first be blinded by the bright light of the fire, confused and disoriented, and would want to return to the familiarity of the shadows on the back wall. If he were led out of the cave and into the sunlight, he would be blinded by the glare of the sun and would require some time to regain his vision and to comprehend what he was seeing. Once he became acquainted with the upper world, if he retuned to the cave, his eyes would once again have to adjust to the darkness. No matter how hard he tried to explain to the other prisoners in the cave what he had witnessed, none of them would comprehend what he was talking about.

What was Plato saying about the nature of reality? Or is he alluding to the attainment of knowledge? That's up to you to figure out, which can be quite a challenge if you're metaphorically shackled up in a cave (or permanently stuck on the couch watching television with a bag of potato chips in your hand), like most people are.

THE UNIVERSE AND REALITY

Has the universe always existed? Or was it created last week? And if so, who made the universe? The Chinese? Or is the universe really just an illusion planted in our minds, like Saddam Hussein's weapons of mass destruction? Does the universe go on forever? Or does it end about a mile down the road? And if the world really does exist, is the fabric of the universe machine washable or permanent press?

The Ancient Jews (circa 1900 BCE)

God, a force beyond the comprehension of mankind with no beginning or end, created the universe and everything in it. And on the seventh day, he took a nap.

Thales (circa 640–circa 546 BCE)

Everything in the universe originated from water. Including crushed ice.

Anaximander (circa 611–circa 547 BCE)

Everything in the universe is made from "the Infinite," a living mass that contains motion, which eventually broke off pieces that became objects and things. Eventually, the broken pieces will come back together again—like one big cosmic jigsaw puzzle.

Anaximines of Miletus (sixth century BCE)

Everything in the universe is made from air. Apparently, Anaximines was made of hot air.

Pythagoras (580–500 BCE)

Everything in the universe is made of numbers. And life is one big math quiz.

Xenophanes (circa 570–475 BCE)

The universe is an unchangeable solid mass. Sort of like Elizabeth Taylor.

Heraclitus (circa 535–circa 475 BCE)

Everything in the universe is made of fire, and the only constant in the universe is perpetual change, caused by "strife." That could explain the high divorce rate.

Anaxagoras (circa 500–428 BCE)

Millions of unchangeable elements combine and separate to form things. In other words, the universe is a vast Lego set with a mind of its own.

Empedocles (circa 495–circa 435 BCE)

Everything in universe is composed of four root elements: earth, air, fire, and water. Love causes these four elements to mingle together to create other things. Hate causes these things to break apart and hire attorneys.

Democritus (460–370 BCE)

Infinitesimal atoms combine in different ways and quantities to form things. All atoms are alike, contain motion, and are indestructible. Well, not quite.

Plato (circa 427–circa 347 BCE)

The material world is a copy of a real world of ideas, forms, or "eternal patterns." The universe is the result of the influence of the world of ideas upon matter. The "Demiurge" was the architect who impressed his world of ideas upon matter. The imperfections in the material world result from the inability to accurately impress ideas upon matter. Ever try baking the perfect German chocolate cake?

Aristotle (384–322 BCE)

Ideas do not exist in a spiritual world separate from the material world we inhabit, but instead ideas are contained within matter and the two are inseparable. Matter constantly strives to take on form. Matter seeks to realize itself, to become something, and this causes all motion in the universe. The tree aspires to be a table, the apple aspires to be applesauce, the uranium aspires to be a thermonuclear bomb.

The Skeptics (circa fourth century BCE)

The preponderance of so many different theories regarding the makeup of the universe implies that man is incapable of discovering the origins or essence of the universe and that all attempts to do so are futile. So don't worry your pretty little head about it.

Epicurus (circa 342–270 BCE)

Made from atoms, the universe came together by pure chance. Hey, anything's possible.

The Stoics (circa third century BCE)

The universe is composed of force and matter, united in every object. Force is composed of fine-grained bodies, while matter is composed of coarse, formless bodies. Together, all the forces in the universe form a collective force which is the living soul of the living universe. This soul is fire, and from this fire arose air, water, and earth—the four basic building blocks for everything else in the universe. Any questions?

Philo (circa 20 circa–circa 50 CE)

Attempting to reconcile Judaism with Plato's philosophy, Philo taught that "Logos" (one of many emanations from God) forged matter into everything in the universe, copying an idea from the mind of God, who said, "Let there be Plato."

Plotinus (circa 205–270)

Both mind and matter emanated from God, and mind shaped matter into the universe—simultaneously creating the cliché "mind over matter."

St. Augustine (354–430)

God created matter out of nothing, then impressed the ideas in his mind on matter to create the universe. All ideas impressed upon matter, being divine, strive to return to God, but are held back by matter. Kind of like the caterpillar inside a Mexican jumping bean.

John Scottus Erigena (circa 815–circa 877)

God created the universe "out of himself, the causeless first cause." Based on a pattern in his mind, God radiated the world as "an expression of the thought of God," which remains in unity with God. This makes a lot more sense after a few hits from a bong.

Thomas Aquinas (circa 1225–1274)

Universal ideas exist in individual objects, making them what they are. These universal ideas exist in the mind of God, who impressed them upon matter, which God created out of nothing. So if an apple is imbued with the idea that it is an apple, does the same go for a candy apple?

Meister Eckhart (circa 1260–circa 1327)

God, the home of eternal ideas, created the world out of nothing and remains distinct from the world. Like a Hollywood producer watching his own B–movie.

John Duns Scotus (circa 1265–circa 1308)

Everything in the world is the result of the union of form (or ideas in God's mind) and matter. Except manmade lakes.

William of Occam (circa 1300–1349)

The only reality in the universe is objects and things. Ideas and universal forms exist only in the mind of man. In other words, guys, you're over–thinking this whole thing.

Ludovico Vives (1492–1540)

Abandon what philosophers of the past said about the universe, and instead, experience the universe for yourself and draw your own conclusions. You're on your own, bub.

Francis Bacon (1561–1626)

The only things that exist in the universe are individual bodies, which act according to fixed laws, which, if understood, explain how the universe works and can be controlled. But you'll have to figure out those laws for yourself.

Galileo Galilei (1564–1642)

The movement of atoms causes all change in the universe. Not bad considering the existence of atoms wasn't proven until several centuries after Galileo's death.

Tommaso Campanella (1568–1639)

Nature is a revelation of God, the creative mind from which the world emanated—along with Excedrin Headache #27.

Thomas Hobbes (1588–1679)

The universe is a world of bodies set in motion in space by God, and these bodies each have certain characteristics (called "accidents"). One body acts upon another body, destroying or creating accidents, in accord with the law of cause and effect. So make sure you have both collision and comprehensive insurance.

René Descartes (1596–1650)

Everything in nature can be explained mathematically. The universe is composed of two independent substances created by God: mind and body. There is no empty space or vacuum in the universe, and bodies can be split infinitely into smaller particles. God gave the world a finite amount of constant motion, which can be neither created nor destroyed, and the laws of nature are the laws of motion. It's as simple as $x = y^3 + z^5$.

Arnold Guelincx (1624–1669)

God possesses knowledge of the universe, and people can know only themselves—with the possible exception of Sir Isaac Newton, Galileo Galilei, and Albert Einstein.

Benedict Spinoza (1632–1677)

Every individual thing in the universe is a part of God, and all things are made from the same basic substance. This basic substance is infinite, creates itself, determines itself without limitation, and tends to stain carpeting.

John Locke (1632–1704)

All knowledge originates from impressions made on our senses, and the source of these impressions is the universe. Although we cannot be completely sure that the material universe exists, it seems probable. If the world does exist, it is made up of two types of substances: bodies and souls. Neither are hand washable.

Nicolas Malebranche (1638–1715)

We cannot hope to understand the workings of the universe, all our ideas about the world were instilled in our minds by God, and we cannot possibly know if we are experiencing an actual material world or merely ideas of a material world placed in our heads. Have a nice day!

Gottfreid Wilhelm Leibniz (1646–1716)

The universe is composed of an infinite number of monads or force–atoms, which have varying degrees of clarity, the clearest monads being God. Each individual monad contains an entire universe, and monads work together harmoniously, making the universe a dynamic, living entity. Ah, introducing the new, improved atom—now with a mind of its own.

George Berkeley (1685–1753)

We cannot prove that a material world exists, but we can prove that we possess ideas and experience sensations. The sensations and ideas we experience are caused by God. Although we cannot perceive God, we can perceive the effects of God, through our ideas. Material objects exist only as ideas perceived by the mind or in the mind of God. So for all we know, like the characters in the movie *The Matrix*, we're all hooked up to a complex machine that gives us the mental illusion that we are living a material existence, while the machine feeds on our life essence to fuel its crusade to dominate the material world.

David Hume (1711–1776)

Only things that are perceived exist. Ideas stream through our minds, without any provable cause, and we cannot prove the existence of the material world outside our minds. Since we are unable to prove that God exists, if no one is present to perceive the existence of an object, the object does not exist. If our ideas are not caused by the material world, then we are merely prisoners of our own minds. In other words, you may be nothing more than a brain in a jar of raspberry-flavored formaldehyde, so when you leave the bathroom and close the door behind you, nothing in the bathroom exists anymore, which means, gentlemen, there's no need to put down the seat.

Thomas Reid (1710–1796)

Common sense dictates that the material world exists and causes our sensations and ideas, which correspond to the world. Objects in the material world exist regardless of our ideas about them. So it's safe to keep your money in the bank, because when you return, the bank will still be there.

Immanuel Kant (1724–1804)

Our minds simply interpret our perception of the outside world, so we cannot possibly fathom the universe that exists beyond our thought process. For Kant, there are two universes: the "phenomenal" universe that we experience, and the "noumenal" universe that we create in our minds. Despite our experiences to the contrary, to preserve our moral integrity, we must have reason to believe that the world has no beginning in time, that bodies can be divided infinitely, that we have free will, and that God created everything. Otherwise, if you lose your umbrella, no one will return it to the lost-and-found.

Johann Gottlieb Fichte (1762–1814)

Although everything in the world appears to be material, everything in the universe is actually spirit, produced by and linked to the absolute, eternal ego (or God), which intentionally places limitations upon itself, compelling itself to struggle to exercise its freedom and become conscious of itself—making God the ultimate over-achiever.

Georg Wilhelm Friedrich Hegel (1770–1831)

Everything in the universe is a thought process, evolving from mind to nature, from less clear to more clear. The thinking process of the universe develops the same as the human thinking process—from "thesis" to "antithesis" to "synthesis"—until the universe goes senile and can't remember what it's doing here.

Friedrich Wilhelm Joseph Schelling (1775–1854)

Everything in the universe is one omnipresent spirit that is unconscious of itself in nature but has achieved self–consciousness through man, the Jiminy Cricket of the universe.

Johann Friedrich Herbart (1776–1841)

The universe is made up of a huge number of "reals"—static, unchange-able, indivisible substances that do not extend into time or space. Bodies are composed of reals, and all reals strive for self–preservation. Really.

Arthur Schopenhauer (1788–1860)

"Will" caused everything in the universe to come into being, and this will is a thing unto itself. Well, if nothing else, that explains the phrase "God willing."

Gustav Theodor Fechner (1801–1887)

Just as the human body has a soul, the material world is the body of the universe, and God is the soul of that body. So please don't touch the universe where it doesn't wish to be touched.

John Stuart Mill (1806–1873)

All we can know for certain are our ideas, but the cause of our perceptions is a genuine material world distinct from our ideas and experiences. The universe is ruled by law and order, and we can rely on certain sequences of events, like the moment you sit down at the dinner table, the telephone will ring, and if you answer it, a telemarketer will tell you that you've won a weekend in Idaho Falls if you agree to attend a timeshare seminar.

Rudolf Hermann Lotze (1817–1881)

An eternal soul or mind created the mechanical world of perception, which adheres to physical and chemical laws. Or maybe my malaria is just flaring up again.

Herbert Spencer (1820–1903)

All we can know for certain are phenomena, but the cause of these events—the Absolute Being—is beyond our comprehension. The phenomena, however, are the knowable inner and outer expressions of the unknowable Absolute Being, and these expressions follow the laws of evolution. So, by studying the shadows of the bunny on the wall, we can draw a few conclusions, but we'll never truly know whose hand is making them or why.

William James (1842–1910)

The existence of a spiritual world that causes experiences is possible, but we cannot experience its existence and therefore cannot know anything about it. A theory of the universe must take into account moral responsibility and freedom of action; otherwise, you won't respect me in the morning.

Josiah Royce (1855–1916)

The universe is a unified self-conscious Being. We are all parts of the thinking universe, a spiritual rather than material world. Matter does not exist. What we perceive as matter are the ideas of the universe, the Absolute, God. But if you break anything, you have to buy it.

Henri Bergson (1859–1941)

The universe is a living thing continually growing through a process of "creative evolution." To understand the universe, we must immerse ourselves in it and use our intuition to see that the creative force of the universe has reinvented itself through matter, emerging as mankind. No delusions of grandeur here.

John Dewey (1859–1952)

The universe is a growing, evolving entity, forever being enriched. Whether an external spiritual world exists makes no difference. All we can know for certain is the universe of our experience, and we should concentrate our energies on better understanding it. So stop daydreaming and do your goddamn homework.

George Santayana (1863–1952)

We can know the substance of the universe through experience—by discovering the laws of science. But that doesn't make it any easier to scrape it off your shoes.

The World According to *Animal House*

At the home of an English professor (played by Donald Sutherland), newly initiated Delta fraternity brother Larry Kruger (played by Tom Hulce) smokes marijuana for the first time, weary that the drug may turn him psycho. While stoned, Larry philosophizes with his professor and realizes that our solar system could be one atom in the fingernail of another giant being, which means that one atom in his own fingernail could contain an infinitesimal solar system. Awed by his drug inspired insight, Larry inquires if he can buy some pot from his professor.

ZENO'S PARADOXES

Zeno of Elea (circa 490–circa 430 BCE) proved, through his paradoxes, that logic can rationally lead to an absurd conclusion, without anyone being able to find fault with the logical argument.

The Dichotomy Paradox

To finish a race, a runner must first cross half the distance, then half the remaining distance, then half of that remaining distance, and so on. Finishing the race involves crossing an infinite number of points, but logic suggests that an infinite number of points cannot be crossed in a finite amount of time.

Similarly, before a runner can run a certain distance, he must run half the distance. Before he can complete half the course, he must complete a quarter of the course. Before he can finish a quarter of the distance, he must finish an eighth of the distance, and so on. The runner must complete an infinite number of events, which requires an infinite amount of time, therefore the runner will never be able to start the race because motion is impossible.

Achilles and the Tortoise Paradox

Achilles and a tortoise decide to have a race for one hundred yards. Since Achilles can run twice as fast as the tortoise, he gives the tortoise a head start of fifty yards. When Achilles reaches the fifty yard mark, the tortoise reaches the seventy-five yard mark. When Achilles reaches the seventy-five yard mark, the tortoise reaches the 87.5 yard mark. Every time Achilles reaches the tortoise's last mark, the tortoise has moved ahead by half that distance. And so, Achilles will never catch up with the tortoise, and neither Achilles nor the tortoise will ever reach the finish line.

The Arrow Paradox

If an archer shoots an arrow at a target, at every moment in time during its flight, the arrow is located at a specific position. At the smallest instant of time, the arrow is at rest during that instant. The arrow is also at rest during every sequential instant. Therefore, the arrow is always at rest and does not move. Motion is impossible and merely an illusion.

The Stadium Paradox

In three rows of seats at a stadium, three people are seated in three rows of seats, just like the first position below.

First Position				**Second Position**		
(Row 1)	0 0 0			(Row 1)	0 0 0	
(Row 2)	0 0 0			(Row 2)	0 0 0	
(Row 3)	0 0 0			(Row 3)	0 0 0	

The people in Row 1 remain seated, and the people in rows B and C stand up, move at equal speeds in opposite directions, and sit down, creating the second position. Each person in Row 2 has passed two people in Row 3 and only one person in Row 1. Thus it takes a person in Row 2 twice as long to pass a person in Row 1 as it does to pass a person in Row 3. Yet, the time required for each person in Rows 2 and 3 to reach the position of Row 1 is the equal. Therefore, half the time is equal to twice the time.

How Can You Be In Two Places At Once When You're Not Anywhere At All?

Side 1 of the classic 1969 Firesign Theatre comedy album, *How Can You Be In Two Places At Once When You're Not Anywhere At All?*, opens to find a man called "Babe" buying a car from Ralph Spoilsport. Babe hops in and drives onto the freeway. As Babe talks to himself, adjusting the knobs on the car radio to find a station he likes, we hear the billboards talking as Babe drives by. "Wrong Way." "Entering Freeway." "Emergency Parking Only." "Merging Busses Ahead." "Shadow Valley Condoms: If you lived here you'd be home by now." Babe decides to take the Antelope Freeway, and as he continues talking to himself, the approaching signs announce: "Antelope Freeway, 1 mile." "Antelope Freeway, ½ mile." "Antelope Freeway, ¼ mile." "Antelope Freeway, ⅛ mile." "Antelope Freeway, ¹⁄₁₆ mile." "Antelope Freeway, ¹⁄₃₂ mile." "Antelope Freeway, ¹⁄₆₄ mile." Babe has unwittingly entered Zeno's Paradox, and he never gets to the Antelope Freeway.

The Liar Paradox

True or false: "I am a liar."

This is statement is true only if it is false. And the statement is false only if it is true. Although you may think this paradox is just a goofy joke from junior high school, its origins are traditionally attributed to philosopher and poet Epimenides of Crete (circa sixth century BCE and Greek philosopher Eubulides of Miletus (fourth century BCE).

WHAT IS REALITY?

"What is reality, anyway? Just a collective hunch."

—Lily Tomlin

"Reality is merely an illusion, albeit a very persistent one."

—Albert Einstein

"Reality leaves a lot to the imagination."

—John Lennon

"Reality is something you rise above."

—Liza Minnelli

"Reality is that which, when you stop believing in it, doesn't go away."

—Philip K. Dick

"All is miracle. The stupendous order of nature, the revolution of a hundred millions of worlds around a million of suns, the activity of light, the life of animals, all are grand and perpetual miracles."

—Voltaire

"It's all in the mind, you know?"

—George Harrison

"Few people have the imagination for reality."

—Johann Wolfgang von Goethe

"Humankind cannot stand very much reality."

—T.S. Eliot

"Nothing can be produced out of nothing."

—Diogenes

"Reality, however utopian, is something from which people feel the need of taking pretty frequent holidays."

—Aldous Huxley

"Reality, if rightly interpreted, is grander than fiction."

—Thomas Carlyle

"The difference between fiction and reality? Fiction has to make sense."

—Tom Clancy

"I've wrestled with reality for thirty-five years, Doctor, and I'm happy to state I finally won out over it."

—Jimmy Stewart in *Harvey,* 1950

"Reality is only a Rorschach ink–blot."

—Alan Watts

"What we call reality is only one way of seeing the world, a way that is supported by social consensus."

—Carlos Castaneda

"Love . . . is a living reality."

—Albert Schweitzer

"There is no reality except the one contained within us. That is why so many people live such an unreal life. They take the images outside them for reality and never allow the world within to assert itself."

—Hermann Hesse

"The death of dogma is the birth of reality."

—Immanuel Kant

"The world of reality has its limits; the world of imagination is boundless."

—Jean-Jacques Rousseau

"The permanent temptation of life is to confuse dreams with reality. The permanent defeat of life comes when dreams are surrendered to reality."

—James Michener

"Someone's opinion of you does not have to become your reality."

—Les Brown

"Reality is a sliding door."

—Ralph Waldo Emerson

"Life is not a problem to be solved, but a reality to be experienced."

—Søren Kierkegaard

"I'm not crazy about reality, but it's still the only place to get a decent meal."

—Groucho Marx

Reality According to *The Wizard of Oz*

To leave the Emerald City, Dorothy clicks her ruby slippers together three times and repeats "There's no place like home" until she wakes up to find herself in bed in her room in Kansas, surrounded by Uncle Henry, Aunt Em, the farmhands, and Professor Marvel. Dorothy insists that she was gone for days and days, but Uncle Henry tells Dorothy that she merely experienced a bad dream. Yet Dorothy, convinced by the vividness of her experience, voices her firm belief that Oz is indeed a genuine place.

The ancient Egyptians, Jews, Babylonians, Greeks, and Romans believed that dreams contained divine messages. The Greek philosopher Heraclitus suggested that the human mind creates each person's dream world. But Dorothy Gales of Kansas raises an interesting philosophical question: is reality a dream, or are our dreams reality?

WHAT WERE THEY THINKING?

MAN

Is man the center of the universe, the pinnacle of all creation, the crowning achievement of a God who doesn't seem to be taking any phone calls? Or is man just an insignificant speck of dust in the wind, another inconsequential brick in the wall? Who was right? Kansas? Or Pink Floyd? And does the universe even care who wins the battle of the bands?

Thales (circa 640–circa 546 BCE)
Man is made of water, just like everything else in the universe, and eventually returns to water. So, hypothetically, that glass of water could be your grandmother.

Heraclitus (circa 535–circa 475 BCE)
Man is subject to the laws of the universe, and as a part of nature, cannot escape this world. Obviously, Heraclitus had no clue that one day astronauts would be living in a tin can circling the earth.

Protagoras (fifth century BCE)

Man is the center of the universe, unfettered by the laws of the universe and free to determine his own fate and mold the world to satisfy his desires. Unless that man gets struck by lightening, swallowed by a tsunami, washed away by a hurricane, or buried in hot lava by a volcano.

Socrates (469–399 BCE)

Man is the center of everything worth thinking about, and knowing how to live morally and ethically is more important than discovering the origins of the universe. So mind your manners or else we're not going to discuss the Big Bang.

Plato (circa 427–circa 347 BCE)

Man is a creature of the universe capable of comprehending the true nature of the universe and, therefore, has a unique place in the universe. Man's soul must rise above the body and dwell in a realm of mind to connect with the reality of ideas. Wow, it's Lucy in the Sky with Diamonds!

Aristotle (384–322 BCE)

Man's power to think creatively is the spark of the divine in man. This makes man God's highest creation, capable of partaking in the divinity of the universe. Man can sculpt masterpieces from marble, build magnificent cathedrals, or invent the Thigh Master.

The Stoics (circa third century BCE)

Man should submit himself to the law of the universe and live according to nature, falling into his proper place in the divine order. Hup, two, three, four. Hup, two, three, four.

St. Augustine (354–430)

God created everything in the universe and God's supreme creation is man, a union of body and soul. Man spends his life trying to return to God, and the only way to achieve this redemption is through Jesus Christ, a conduit back to God, provided by God. Or you can have what's behind Door #2.

John Scotus Erigena (circa 815–circa 877)

God, who created the universe and is the universe, created man with the free will to turn away from God. Go ahead. Run away from home. See if I care.

Peter Abelard (1079–1142)

The universe is an expression of God's essence, and therefore a spark of God is in man and will eventually return to the totality of God. In the end, man is just an empty soda bottle, and God wants his nickel deposit back.

Thomas Aquinas (circa 1225–1274)

Man, having been created by God, contains a spark of the divine, but man, being both matter and spirit, is debased by his physical desires and must seek redemption to be reunited with God. So you might want to consider donating that vibrator to the Salvation Army.

Francis Bacon (1561–1626)

Religious ideas and scientific discoveries often contradict each other, but man is obligated to believe both. That's why your head feels like it's going to explode.

Thomas Hobbes (1588–1679)

Since everything in the universe is matter in motion, man must understand the laws of motion to comprehend the universe and use these laws to his benefit. Unless you'd rather take a nap.

René Descartes (1596–1650)

Man, being of both mind and matter, must reconcile his spiritual side with the mechanical laws of nature. Or you can wet your pants. It's your choice.

Benedict Spinoza (1632–1677)

Everything in the universe is divine substance; therefore, man is a form of God with a mode of matter (or body) and a mode of mind (or thought). In man, unlike other objects or animals, the mode of mind is conscious of itself—unless you're a used car salesman.

John Locke (1632–1704)

Man, experiencing the world through his senses, is a union of mind and body, two parts that interact with each other, but remain independent of each other. God gave man reason as the ultimate test of everything in the universe, to see if man could reason that God and an outer world exist. In short, Dr. Frankenstein gave life to the creature and then hid in a closet to see if the creature could figure out who created him and why.

Gottfried Wilhelm Leibniz (1646–1716)

Man, like everything in the universe, is made from monads acting in harmony with each other and controlled by a central monad or soul. God created the universe and then backed off, allowing the monads to do their own thing, in accord with the laws of nature. Although man is subject to the confines of the universe and its mechanical laws, he can still dance the Macarena.

George Berkeley (1685–1753)

The material universe does not exist. The world exists only when perceived by the mind of man, and those perceptions are planted in our heads by the mind of God. So you might as well call the office tomorrow morning and tell them you're not coming in because reality is an illusion.

David Hume (1711–1776)

All we know for certain is that the universe exists in the mind of man, and we cannot know for certain if these ideas are caused by the existence of an actual material world or if they are planted in our heads by God. Therefore, says Hume, we cannot even be certain if we physically exist. The individual could, after all, be nothing more than a string of ideas floating through space. In other words, there's really no need to make your bed every morning.

Jean-Jacques Rousseau (1712–1778)

Man must escape from the stifling bonds of science, which define him as a machine in a mechanical universe, and instead embrace his true nature as a feeling, sensitive creature. Immerse yourself in a soothing bubble bath, add a few drops of eucalyptus oil, light some scented candles, put on some soft music, and get in touch with the true essence of your existence.

Immanuel Kant (1724–1804)

Man, possessing the ability to reason, can conceptualize an outer world, God, freedom, and the immortality of his own soul. The belief in these ideas compels man to act with integrity and dignity, enabling him to take control of his own destiny and create a world of values by embracing the moral truths within himself. In other words, man acts ethically, but only if he believes in a lot of hooey.

Johann Gottlieb Fichte (1762–1814)

Life has value and meaning only if we accept the notion that man is free to do as he chooses, unfettered by predetermined events. As part of the absolute ego of the universe, which unfolds freely and creatively with self–determination, man is the supreme expression of this absolute ego. So do whatever you damn well please.

Friederich Ernst Daniel Schleiermacher (1768–1834

God, the guiding creative force in the universe, created man to help the universe realize itself and to push the limits of the universe's creative ability—by polluting the skies and melting the polar ice caps.

Friedrich Wilhelm Joseph Schelling (1775–1854)

The universe, including man, is a living, creative, evolving work of art by a divine artist—with man as an intricate part of the whole. It's just not clear whether this work of art is rococo, cubism, abstract expressionism, or surrealism.

Georg Wilhelm Friedrich Hegel (1770–1831)

Man is a microcosm of the universe. Thoughts in the human mind evolve from "thesis" to "antithesis" to "synthesis" in a never–ending continuum. The universe evolves in the same way, but on a much larger scale. Man uses ideas to mold matter, just as the divine intelligence uses ideas to shape the universe. In short, life is a never–ending high school debate.

Johann Friedrich Herbart (1776–1841)

Man, like the universe, is a machine regulated by unalterable laws. Everything in the universe, including the mind of man, is composed of "reals," units that mingle and separate according to fixed laws of nature. Man's thought process is therefore mechanical, the predictable interaction of reals. By understanding the laws governing reals, we can ultimately control people—using peer pressure and slick television commercials to persuade them to buy gas–guzzling SUVs and Hummers so that the oil industry can stage an energy crisis and rake in billions.

Arthur Schopenhauer (1788–1860)

Man is driven by will, the primary force of the universe, but man's will is supreme and conscious of itself, making man a microcosm of the universe . . . . if you will.

Auguste Comte (1798–1857)

Man can never know the inner essence of the universe or man. However, by observing and experiencing various phenomena, man discovers regularities and the consequences of various actions and learns how to control these phenomena or use them to his advantage. Hmmm, ever notice that your head feels a lot better when you stop banging it against a wall?

John Stuart Mill (1806–1873)

Man can find regularities within the universe by using a logical method of deduction to determine that a particular action consistently causes the same effect. These predictable sequences, Mill noted, can be found both in the universe and in man. However, the innumerable factors to be considered with man make predicting his actions enormously difficult—although horoscope columnists always seem to hit the nail on the head.

Rudolf Hermann Lotze (1817–1881)

Man, with his self–conscious mind, is the ultimate creation produced by the creative intelligence that is the universe. Second place goes to the baboon.

Herbert Spencer (1820–1903)

Man is a result of the evolutionary development of the universe, and mankind continues evolving in this on-going process. His crowning achievement thus far? The Ziploc Storage Bag.

William James (1842–1910)

Our theory of the universe is based purely on our experience and our perspective as human beings. Therefore man is the center of the universe because we interpret the universe solely through the prism of the human experience. In all likelihood, we'd have a totally different perspective on the universe if we were houseflies.

Friedrich Nietzsche (1844–1900)

The essence of man is the will to power, an innate determination that cares nothing about consequences to others. This will to power is also the basic force in the universe, which drives on without any concern for or knowledge of man's existence. Man doesn't give a flying fuck about his fellow man, the universe doesn't give a flying fuck about man, and reading Nietzsche makes you feel like . . . aw, who gives a flying fuck?

John Dewey (1859–1952)

Man is both a creation of the evolutionary process and a part of the evolutionary process in which the universe achieves self–consciousness. Man can understand the universe only in terms of his experience, which is limited to fifth-row balcony seats.

Bertrand Russell (1872–1970)

Man is an insignificant part of the vast mathematical machine of a world governed by consistent, inescapable scientific laws. In the grand scheme of things, mankind's existence is brief and inconsequential, and frankly, the universe doesn't give a damn.

Martin Heidegger (1899–1976)

Man is the only creature that can ponder its own existence, achieve awareness of its connection to the existence of the universe, and thus rise above all other beings. Only then does man attain his existential authenticity—and the chance to win a free in–home estimate for resurfacing the kitchen cabinets.

Jean–Paul Sartre (1905–1980)

God does not exist, so man is not imbued with a divine spark. Instead, man is a continually evolving creature who must perpetually determine what he is and forever struggle to make something of himself. Unless you're content pumping Slurpees at the 7–Eleven.

The Fred School of Philosophy

Why do so many philosophers share the name Fred?

- Friedrich Wilhelm Joseph Schelling
- Friederich Ernst Daniel Schleiermacher
- Georg Wilhelm Friedrich Hegel
- Johann Friedrich Herbart
- Friedrich Nietzsche

THINKERS AND STINKERS

CRAZY OVER CONFUCIUS

- Legend holds that Chinese philosopher Confucius (circa 551–circa 479 BCE) whose given name was K'ung Ch'iu, grew up in the duchy of Lu, (near the present-day town of Qufu in southeastern Shandong) in an impoverished family and was forced to take jobs accounting and caring for livestock.

- The name Confucius is the Latin version of the Chinese name K'ung F–tzu, which means "Great Master K'ung."

- Confucius was the first person in recorded history to advocate the Golden Rule, which he stated as, "Do not do to others what you would not want done to yourself."

- Appointed Minister of Public Works and then Minister of Crime, Confucius was subsequently forced to leave office and go into exile. Confucius left Lu and, together with his disciples, traveled in the states of Wei, Song, Chen, Cai, and Chu, purportedly seeking a position as an adviser to a ruler who might put into practice his ideas for reforming society—without any success.

- The teachings of Confucius are contained in *The Analects,* a collection of twenty books, written by his disciples.

- Apparently Confucius died at the age of seventy-two, a number with magical significance in early Chinese literature.

Confucius Condensed ➡ ◀

One of the most important philosophers in China, Confucius believed that a civilized society can survive only if its citizens adhere to definite rules of moral conduct that can be written concisely in fortune cookies.

WHAT CONFUCIUS SAID

"The superior man acts before he speaks, and afterwards speaks according to his action."

"The gem cannot be polished without friction, nor man perfected without trials."

"When anger rises, think of the consequences."

"It is not failure of others to appreciate your abilities that should trouble you, but rather your failure to appreciate theirs."

"If you have made a mistake, do not be afraid of admitting the fact and amending your ways."

"Everything has its beauty, but not everyone sees it."

"It is only the wisest and the stupidest that cannot change."

"The gentleman prefers to be slow in word but diligent in action."

"A gentleman considers what is right; the vulgar consider what will pay."

"To know what is right and not to do it is the worst cowardice."

"Settle one difficulty, and you keep a hundred away."

"It does not matter how slowly you go, as long as you do not stop."

"One who has accumulated virtue will certainly also possess eloquence; but he who has eloquence does not necessarily possess virtue."

"Attack the evil that is within yourself, rather than attacking the evil that is in others."

"The real fault is to have faults and not try to mend them."

"To be wronged is nothing, unless you continue to remember it."

"Heaven means to be one with God."

"Shall I teach you what knowledge is? When you know a thing, to recognize that you know it, and when you do not know a thing, to recognize that you do not know it. That is knowledge."

"When we see men of worth, we should think how we may learn to equal them. When we see men of a contrary character, we should turn inward and examine ourselves."

"Better a diamond with a flaw than a pebble without."

"You judge yourself by what you think you can achieve, others judge you by what you have achieved."

"Real knowledge is to know the extent of one's ignorance."

"A man who has committed a mistake and doesn't correct it, is committing another mistake."

"The cautious seldom err."

"The gentleman can see a question from all sides without bias. The small man is biased and can see a question only from one side."

"Our greatest glory is not in never failing, but in rising every time we fail."

"He who conquers himself is the mightiest warrior."

"Silence is a friend who will never betray."

"The gentleman thinks always of virtue; the common man thinks of comfort."

"To understand yourself is the key to wisdom."

"Have no friends not equal to yourself."

"The gentle man is satisfied and composed; the mean man is always full of distress."

"The man who in the view of gain thinks of righteousness; who in the view of danger is prepared to give up his life; and who does not forget an old agreement however far back it extends—such a man may be reckoned a complete man."

"Recompense injury with justice, and recompense kindness with kindness."

"What the gentleman seeks is in himself. What the mean man seeks is in others."

I am

"I think, therefore I am."
—René Descartes

"I am what I do."
—Martin Buber

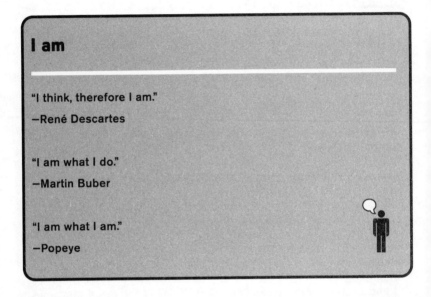

"I am what I am."
—Popeye

The Phenomenology of *Dark Star*

In the 1974 movie *Dark Star,* directed by John Carpenter, a malfunction aboard a rundown spaceship accidentally initiates the launch sequence of the ship's thermostellar nuclear bombs. When computerized Bomb #20 refuses to disarm itself and return to the bomb bay, the ship's commander, Lt. Doolittle, dons a spacesuit and goes for spacewalk to teach Bomb #20 some phenomenology. He asks the bomb how it knows that it exists, and the bomb replies with the words of Descartes, "I think, therefore I am." Doolittle attempts to convince the bomb that the world outside its own thought processes is unknowable because all that the bomb knows about the outside world is sensory data relayed through a stream of electrical impulses that stimulate its computing center. The bomb admits that it cannot be certain that the outside universe truly exists. Acknowledging that its sole purpose is to explode once, the bomb considers whether it wishes to detonate itself based on an order that could very be false data unconnected with outside reality. The bomb mulls this over and concludes that all data it receives from the outside world must be false. Convinced that the only thing that exists is itself, the bomb determines that it must therefore be God, alone in the darkness, so it says "Let There Be Light" and detonates itself.

FREAKY PHILOSOPHERS

That Doggone Diogenes

The Greek philosopher Diogenes (circa 400–325 BCE) dressed like a beggar, lived in an earthenware tub on the grounds of a temple in Athens, and was nicknamed "The Dog." The Greeks called his students the Cynics, from the Greek word *kunikos*, meaning "canine." The students wore the epithet as a badge of honor, seeing themselves as the watchdogs of morality. Diogenes wished to be buried like a dog. Plato described Diogenes as "a Socrates gone mad."

Diogenes is best known for proclaiming himself "a citizen of the world." Legend holds that Alexander the Great went to meet Diogenes and purportedly asked if there was anything the philosopher wanted. "Yes," replied Diogenes, "get out of my sunlight." Admiring the philosopher's candor, Alexander supposedly said, "Were I not Alexander, I would wish to be Diogenes."

Diogenes was buried in Corinth, and his tomb was topped with a carving of a dog.

That Baffling Berkeley

Irish philosopher Bishop George Berkeley (1685–1753) insisted that material objects do not exist unless they are perceived by the senses. Objects continue to exist, he explained, when they are not being observed by humans—because the objects are being observed by God, who is omnipresent, perceiving everything, regardless if humans are present. The continual existence of objects, Berkeley claimed, proves the existence of God. The city of Berkeley, California, is named after George Berkeley.

Night of the Living Jeremy Bentham

British philosopher Jeremy Bentham (1748–1832) insisted that "if all bodies were embalmed, every man might be his own statue." Bentham donated his corpse to University College in London, which he helped found. After using his body for medical research, the college, following instructions in Bentham's will, reconstructed Bentham's skeleton, padded it with straw, gave it a wax head, dressed it in Bentham's clothes, and displayed the "auto–icon" in a glass case. Legend holds that in the minutes of meetings of the college council, Bentham was always recorded as "present, but not voting."

Bentham originally intended for his head to be part of the auto–icon, but the preservation process went awry, giving the face a gruesome expression and prompting the college to substitute a wax head. Legend holds that for years Bentham's real head, with its glass eyes, sat on the floor of the glass case. Purportedly, students from nearby King's College London frequently stole it, and Bentham's actual head was once found in a luggage locker at London's Aberdeen station. Today, Bentham's head sits in the college vaults and his auto-icon is on display in the South Cloisters at University College in London.

Diderot's Dowry

To raise money for a dowry for his daughter, French philosopher Denis Diderot (1713–1784), a leading editor of the French *Encyclopedia* and a prolific writer, sold all the books in his personal library for the equivalent of $3,000 to Empress Catherine II of Russia. Diderot also agreed to serve as custodian of the library for fifty years at an annual salary of the equivalent of $200. Catherine paid Diderot's entire salary in advance.

Flipping Out with John Stuart Mill

British philosopher John Stuart Mill (1806–1873) never attended school. Instead he was home schooled by his father, economist and historian James Mill, who taught his son Greek at the age of 3, Latin, algebra, and geometry at the age of 8, and logic at the age of 12. John Stuart Mill suffered a nervous breakdown at age 20. Scholars estimate that he had an IQ of 190.

The Opposite Philosophy

The word *epicure,* meaning a person who overindulges in fine food and drink, stems from the name of the Greek philosopher Epicurus (circa 342–270 BCE) who actually advocated moderation in seeking pleasure, noting that overindulgence often leads to pain. The philosophy of Epicurus, known as hedonism, stressed seeking pleasure through temperance, courage, and justice. In the seventeenth and eighteenth centuries, the French leisure class embraced a warped version of hedonism to validate their self-indulgent lifestyles—giving the word *epicure* its backwards, modern-day meaning.

The Friendly Philosopher

French philosopher Bernard de Fontenelle (1657–1757), who lived to be one-hundred years old, never married and never had a friend.

Cicero and the Chickpea

The name of the great Roman orator and statesman Marcus Tullius Cicero (106–43 BCE) is derived from the Latin word *cicer*, meaning "chuckpea." According to the Greek biographer Plutarch, the name Cicero was bestowed upon one of Cicero's ancestors, whose nose had a small, bulbous cleft tip that resembled a chickpea.

Till Death Do Us Part

German philosopher Johann Gottlieb Fichte (1762–1814) was buried near the grave of fellow German philosopher Georg Wilhelm Friedrich Hegel (1770–1831), by his own request.

WHO DOES MAN THINK HE IS ANYWAY?

"Man is the most intelligent of the animals—and the most silly."

—Diogenes

"Man—a creature made at the end of the week's work when God was tired."

—Mark Twain

"We must laugh at man to avoid crying for him."

—Napoleon Bonaparte

"Our humanity were a poor thing were it not for the divinity which stirs within us."

—Francis Bacon

"The more humanity advances, the more it is degraded."

—Gustave Flaubert

"Apart from man, no being wonders at its own existence."

—Arthur Schopenhauer

"Man with all his noble qualities . . . still bears in his bodily frame the indelible stamp of his lowly origin."

—Charles Darwin

"I know of no more encouraging fact than the unquestionable ability of man to elevate his life by a conscious endeavor."

—Henry David Thoreau

"I sometimes think that God in creating man somewhat overestimated his ability."

—Oscar Wilde

"I do not understand what the man who is happy wants in order to be happier."

—Marcus Tullius Cicero

"The significance of man is that he is insignificant and is aware of it."

—Carl Becker

"Cursed is every one who places his hope in man."

—St. Augustine

"I love mankind. It's people I can't stand."

—Linus in *Peanuts*

"Too bad that all the people who know how to run the country are busy driving taxicabs and cutting hair."

—George Burns

"God must love the common man, he made so many of them."

—Abraham Lincoln

"The human body is the best picture of the human soul."

—Ludwig Wittgenstein

"Just because some of us can read and write and do a little math, that doesn't mean we deserve to conquer the universe."

—Kurt Vonnegut

"Mankind is divisible into two great classes: hosts and guests."

—Sir Max Beerbohm

"When a true genius appears in this world, you may know him by this sign, that the dunces are all in confederacy against him."

—Jonathan Swift

"We spend the first twelve months of our children's lives teaching them to walk and talk and the next twelve telling them to sit down and shut up."

—Phyllis Diller

"Whenever people agree with me I always feel I must be wrong."

—Oscar Wilde

GOOD VERSUS EVIL

What is good? What is evil? Are they absolute constants in the universe? Does disco suck? Or in retrospect, when compared with rap, is it really good? And when compared with the incessant pounding of a jackhammer, does Snoop Doggy Dog sound like Frank Sinatra? Do good and bad depend upon the impact an action has on society? If a horrible movie like *Police Academy 7* makes $70 million at the box office, does that make it good?

Heraclitus (circa 535–circa 475 BCE)

People see good and evil, but God, looking at the big picture, sees a harmonious universe in which everything is fair and just. Man struggles to see the world as a balanced combination of good and bad, but a 24-hour bout with Montezuma's Revenge can really taint your outlook on life.

Democritus (460–370 BCE)

The goal of life is happiness, an inner peace achieved by harmonizing the soul, by balancing life through reflection and reason, by always desiring to do good, and by hiring a really good accountant to do your tax returns.

The Sophists (fifth century BCE)

Each individual has the right to define good and evil for himself. Moral laws go in and out of style, like fashion, so the individual must think for himself to develop a personal code of right and wrong. Still, everyone should avoid wearing a polka–dot shirt with plaid pants.

Socrates (469–399 BCE)

The highest good is knowledge, which enables man to choose the morally and ethically correct course of action. Thus, man must forever seek knowledge—and a halfway decent pastrami sandwich.

Plato (circa 427–circa 347 BCE)

Reason is the ultimate good, culminating in the release of the soul from the body to forever contemplate the realm of ideas. In the meantime, man can enjoy a good life on earth by using reason to control his appetite and will, making him wise, courageous, happy, and an incredible bore at cocktail parties.

Aristotle (384–322 BCE)

The highest good is self–realization, and man attains happiness by achieving the full capacity of his reason and gaining balanced control of his emotions, desires, and appetites. The man who realizes the full potential of his reason becomes naturally virtuous, considerate, and caring—from the depth of his soul. He also tends to get all the hot babes.

Epicurus (circa 342–270 BCE)

The ultimate goal of life is pleasure, which brings happiness for all. We can free ourselves from the pain of any desire by fulfilling that desire. However, since immediate pleasure can result in pain and suffering, we must consider the consequences before indulging in pleasurable activities. So don't eat that entire box of doughnuts yourself.

The Stoics (circa third century BCE)

To achieve the highest good, man must act in harmony with the universe, using reason to rule his actions and abiding by the laws of nature. So please, keep off the grass.

Philo (circa 20 circa–circa 50 BCE)

God is the source of all good, and matter is the source of all evil. Therefore, the human soul is good, but the human body is evil. Man must free his soul from the evils of the human body and return to God. Sorry fellas, that means no more *Girls Gone Wild.*

St. Augustine (354–430)

Everything in the universe is good—even evil. God created evil to complete the picture, just as an artist uses shadows to paint a masterpiece. Evil is merely the absence of good, and without evil, we would have no way to appreciate or understand good. But do we really need hemorrhoids to better appreciate the sphincter?

Peter Abelard (1079–1142)

An act can only be judged right or wrong based on the intention of the person committing the act. Therefore, if Robin Hood breaks into your home, ties you to a chair, steals your brand–new wide–screen plasma television screen, and donates it to an orphanage, he's not a criminal.

Thomas Aquinas (circa 1225–1274)

God created everything in the universe for a purpose, and realizing your purpose in life and fulfilling it is the highest act of goodness, because doing so proclaims God's goodness. An act that results in good consequences is not good if the person committing the act did so with bad intentions. However, a bad act committed with good intentions remains a bad act. The highest good is giving up all worldly goods and devoting oneself to God's service. Please donate your brand–new wide–screen plasma television screen to the orphanage, but make sure you do so with good intentions, otherwise you've committed an evil act.

Meister Eckhart (circa 1260–circa 1327)

Man achieves goodness not by doing good deeds, but by surrendering his individuality and attaining oneness with God. So take off that silly "Habitat for Humanity" T-shirt, don a black frock, and join a monastery.

Thomas Hobbes (1588–1679)

Motion is the primary force in the universe. Motion that generates pleasure is good, and motion that generates pain is evil. Since pleasure and pain are in the eye of the beholder, so are good and evil. So a ride on the Tilt–a–Whirl can be good or evil, depending on whether it makes you puke.

René Descartes (1596–1650)

God intentionally gave man a partial ability to accurately discern between true and false. Evil results when man chooses to pass judgment and take action without sufficient evidence. That's why so many fourth graders got a C on last Thursday's Social Studies quiz.

Benedict Spinoza (1632–1677)

All people strive for self–preservation. Any obstacle to this endeavor is bad, and any help or assistance is good. Man achieves the highest good by recognizing that he, being a mode of God, is doing all of this striving for the benefit of God. Face it, chump, you're just another pod person in *Invasion of the Body Snatchers*.

John Locke (1632–1704)

Our conceptions of good and evil are not God–given, but rather taught to us by our parents or impressed upon us by society. We generally consider things that cause pleasure and happiness to be good, and we deem things that cause pain and suffering to be bad. Unless, of course, you're a sado–masochist.

Gottfried Wilhelm Leibniz (1646–1716)

God created finite beings whose limitations result in suffering and sin, but this evil serves to give emphasis to good. The human soul instinctively knows to seek pleasure and avoid pain, enabling man to discern between good and evil, Coke and Pepsi, cotton and polyester, Macintosh and Windows, Nintendo and Xbox, and paper or plastic.

Jean Jacques Rousseau (1712–1778)

The only truly good thing in the universe is the human will ruled by con-scientiousness or respect for moral law. Still, there's nothing like chocolate–covered strawberries.

Immanuel Kant (1724–1804)

One rule—his "categorical imperative"—provides the criterion to deter-mine right from wrong: "Always act in such a way that the maxim determining your conduct might well become a universal law; act so that you can will that everybody shall follow the principle of your action." And don't forget to floss.

Jeremy Bentham (1748–1832)

The greatest good is the good that affects the greatest number of people, which in turn brings the greatest good to the person committing the act. Even if that act is performed by Carrot Top.

Johann Gottlieb Fichte (1762–1814)

The universe is governed by moral law, and man must exercise his intelligence to discover the moral law that has been instilled within him so that he may continuously strive do what is right. Otherwise, he'll never stop leaving dirty dishes in the sink.

Arthur Schopenhauer (1788–1860)

Will, the fundamental force in the universe, creates the selfish struggle for existence and survival, which causes all evil in the world. Sympathy or pity for others, achieved by realizing that every individual is a part of the universal will, creates good through self–sacrifice. This eternal struggle is best observed at Wal-Mart's Day After Thanksgiving Sale.

John Stuart Mill (1806–1873)

An act can be judged good or bad based on how many people the act affects and to what degree. Also, intellectual good is better than physical good. Unless Pamela Anderson is involved.

Herbert Spencer (1820–1903)

Human conduct continually evolves, and the highest good is enriching the lives of the people both now and in the future—by fortifying Kellogg's Rice Krispies with eight essential vitamins and minerals, for instance.

THINKERS AND STINKERS

BRINGING HOME
THE BACON

- At forty-five years of age, British philosopher Sir Francis Bacon (1561–1626) married fourteen–year–old Alice Barnham.

- Sir Francis Bacon was gay. He remained discreet about his sexual preferences, because at the time homosexuality was a crime punishable by death. In his book *Brief Lives*, biographer John Aubrey wrote that Bacon was a "pederast" (meaning "homosexual") with "ganymedes and favourites." Bacon fancied Welsh serving men, and frequently took his servants as bedfellows.

- Despite any conspiracy theories to the contrary, Sir Francis Bacon did not write any of William Shakespeare's plays or sonnets. No reputable Shakespeare scholar has ever seriously proposed that anyone but William Shakespeare wrote his plays. English philosopher and statesman Francis Bacon was born three years before Shakespeare and died ten years after him, but Bacon was neither a poet nor a playwright.

- Sir Francis Bacon, named Lord Chancellor by King James I, was charged with bribery, found guilty upon his own admission, and sentenced to imprisonment in the Tower of London. After serving four days, Bacon was freed by the King.

- In 1626, sixty-five year-old Francis Bacon, attempting an experiment on preserving meat, stuffed a dead chicken with snow, caught a cold, and died.

Bacon Condensed ➡️⬅️

Although he taught that the universe is governed by fixed mathematical and scientific laws that man has the ability to discover for himself, Bacon believed that ultimately, man has no choice but to surrender to the will of God. So you're damned if you do, and you're damned if you don't.

WHAT BACON SAID (OR BACON BITS)

"A little philosophy inclineth man's mind to atheism, but depth in philosophy bringeth men's minds about to religion."

"The best part of beauty is that which no picture can express."

"If a man will begin with certainties, he shall end in doubts, but if he will be content to begin with doubts, he shall end in certainties."

"If a man be gracious and courteous to strangers, it shows he is a citizen of the world."

"It is as natural to die as to be born; and to a little infant, perhaps, the one is as painful as the other."

"Discretion in speech is more than eloquence."

"Nothing is so terrible but fear itself."

"The fortune which nobody sees makes a person happy and unenvied."

"Imagination was given to man to compensate him for what he is not; a sense of humor to console him for what he is."

"Knowledge is power."

"It is impossible to love and be wise."

"Why should I be angry with a man for loving himself better than me?"

"The more a man drinketh of the world, the more it intoxicateth."

"Nature to be commanded, must be obeyed."

"A wise man will make more opportunities than he finds."

"Man prefers to believe what he prefers to be true."

"The remedy is worse than the disease."

"Wives are young men's mistresses, companions for middle age, and old men's nurses."

HARD-BOILED PHILOSOPHY

The main characters in *film noir* classics, surrendering to a base desire and unable to resist the temptation of a *femme fatale*, often spoke simple yet profound philosophical truisms.

"If you want to play with matches, that's your business. But not in gas–filled rooms."

> —Robert Mitchum in *Angel Face,* 1953

"I don't pray. Kneeling bags my nylons."

> —Jan Sterling in *The Big Carnival,* 1951

QUINN: "Everybody dies. Ben, Shorty, even you."
CHARLEY: "What's the point?"
QUINN: "No point—That's life."

> —William Conrad and John Garfield in *Body and Soul,* 1947

"I know what's going on inside of you, Frank. You're just like any other man, only a little more so."

—Pamela Britton in *D.O.A.*, 1950

"I probably shan't return before dawn. How I detest the dawn. The grass looks like it's been left out all night."

—Clifton Webb in *The Dark Corner*, 1946

"All women are rivals, fundamentally."

—Lew Ayres in *Dark Mirror*, 1946

"That's life. Whichever way you turn, fate sticks out a foot to trip you."

—Tom Neal in *Detour*, 1945

"I ain't interfering with justice, but you cops are interfering with my sleep."

—James Kodl in *The Female Jungle*, 1955

"When I bite a steak, I like it to bite back at me."

—William Bendix in *The Glass Key*, 1942

"I was just getting ready to take my tie off, wondering if I should hang myself with it."

—Robert Mitchum in *His Kind of Woman*, 1951

"Be smart, Charlie. Act dumb."

—Gangster boss in *Hoodlum Empire*, 1952

"In this world you turn the other cheek and you get hit with a lug wrench."

—Brian Donlevy in *Impact*, 1949

"It's better to be a live coward than a dead hero."

—Claire Trevor in *Key Largo*, 1948

"Did I ask to be born? Did I?"

—John Derek in *Knock on Any Door*, 1949

"Most men lead lives of quiet desperation. I can't take quiet desperation."

—Ray Milland in *The Lost Weekend*, 1945

"Personally, I'm convinced that alligators have the right idea. They eat their young."

—Eve Arden in *Mildred Pierce*, 1945

"Sure is remarkable how dying can make a saint of a man."

—Allyn Joslyn, in *Moonrise*, 1949

"If I always knew what I mean, I'd be a genius."

—Dick Powell, in *Murder, My Sweet*, 1944

"You're like a leaf that the wind blows from one gutter to another."

—Robert Mitchum, in *Out of the Past*, 1947

"It looks like I'll spend the rest of my life dead."

—Humphrey Bogart in *The Petrified Forest*, 1936

"Have you ever noticed if for some reason you want to feel completely out of step with the rest of the world, the only thing to do is sit around a cocktail lounge in the afternoon?"

—Lizabeth Scott in *Pitfall*, 1948

"Well, so long, mister. Thanks for the ride, the three cigarettes, and for not laughing at my theories on life."

—John Garfield in *The Postman Always Rings Twice*, 1946

"The difference between the honest and the dishonest is a debatable line. We're suckers if we don't try to cram as much happiness as possible in our brief time, no matter how."

—Joseph Cotton in *The Steel Trap*, 1952

MYRA: "Remember what Nietzsche said—'Live dangerously.'"
LESTER: "You know what happened to Nietzsche."
MYRA: "What?"
LESTER: "He's dead."

—Joan Crawford and Jack Palance, in *Sudden Fear*, 1952

"In Italy, for thirty yeats under the Borgias they had warfare, terror, murder, and bloodshed, but they produced Michelangelo, Leonardo Da Vinci, and the Renaissance. In Switzerland, they had brotherly love, they had five hundred years of democracy and peace—and what did they produce? The cuckoo clock."

—Orson Welles, *in The Third Man*, 1949

THE GOLDEN RULE ACCORDING TO TEN WORLD RELIGIONS

Bahá'í

"Blessed is he who prefers his brother before himself."

—Bahá'u'lláh

Buddhism

"Hurt not others in ways that you yourself would find hurtful."

—Udana–Varga 5:1

Christianity

"So in everything, do to others what you would have them do to you; for this sums up the Law and the Prophets."

—Matthew 7:12

Confucianism

"Do not do to others what you would not want done to yourself."

—Analects 12:2

Hinduism

"This is the sum of duty; do naught onto others what you would not have them do unto you."

—Mahabharata 5:15:17

Islam

"No one of you is a believer until he desires for his brother that which he desires for himself."

—Forty Hadith of an–Nawawi 13

Jainism

"A man should wander about treating all creatures as he himself would be treated. "

—Sutrakritanga 1:11:33

Judaism

"You shall love your neighbor as yourself."

—Leviticus 19:18

Taoism

"Regard your neighbor's gain as your gain, and your neighbor's loss as your own loss."

—Tai Shang Kan Yin P'ien

Zoroastrianism

"That nature alone is good which refrains from doing another whatsoever is not good for itself."

—Dadistan–i–Dinik, 94:5

THE GOLDEN RULE ACCORDING TO TEN PHILOSOPHERS

"Do not do to others that which would anger you if others did it to you."

—Socrates

"May I do to others as I would that they should do unto me."

—Plato

"We should behave to our friends as we would wish our friends to behave to us."

—Aristotle

"In nothing do men more nearly approach the gods than in doing good to their fellow men."

—Marcus Tullius Cicero

"Treat your inferiors as you would be treated by your superiors."

—Lucius Annaeus Seneca

"What you would avoid suffering yourself, seek not to impose on others."

—Epictetus

"Do not that to another, which thou wouldst not have done to thyself."

—Thomas Hobbes

"Desire nothing for yourself, which you do not desire for others."

—Benedict Spinoza

"Always act in such a way that the maxim determining your conduct might well become a universal law."

—Immanuel Kant

"When choosing a course of action, assume all mankind will take you as a model and will make the identical choice in the same situation."

—Jean–Paul Sartre

"IS THE GLASS HALF FULL OR HALF EMPTY?"

Heraclitus (circa 535–circa 475 BCE)

"The glass is completely full. Half with water, half with air."

Zeno of Elea (circa 490–circa 430 BCE)

"The glass can never be half full or half empty."

Socrates (469–399 BCE)

"What do you mean by half?"

Plato (circa 427–circa 347 BCE)

"The glass is a form in the realm of ideas."

Aristotle (384–322 BCE)

"Through logic, we can deduce that the glass is dirty."

Epicurus (circa 342–270 BCE)

"If drinking the amount of water in the glass gives one pleasure, then the glass was half full. If drinking the water does not give one pleasure, then the glass was half empty."

St. Augustine (354–430)

"Experience and logic tell us that the glass is half empty, but divine revelation tells us that the glass is half full."

Thomas Aquinas (circa 1225–1274)

"The glass contains a spark of the divine, which is absolute fullness, but the glass is also made from matter, which is complete emptiness."

Francis Bacon (1561–1626)

"First we must accurately measure how much liquid is in the glass, then we must precisely measure how much total liquid the glass is capable of holding, and then, using mathematics, we must correctly determine if the amount of liquid in the glass is indisputably half the amount of liquid that the glass is capable of holding."

René Descartes (1596–1650)

"I drink, therefore the glass is now empty."

Benedict Spinoza (1632–1677)

"The glass and its contents are divine substance, which is absolute fullness."

John Locke (1632–1704)

"Reason tells us that we perceive a glass that seems to exist in the material world, but we cannot be certain whether it truly exists, or if it is half full or half empty."

Gottfried Wilhelm Leibniz (1646–1716)

"The glass, composed of monads, contains water composed of monads and air composed of monads, so that glass is filled with monads."

George Berkeley (1685–1753)

"The idea of the glass in our mind is caused by God and exists spiritually, not materially. Therefore, its fullness or emptiness is immaterial."

David Hume (1711–1776)

"We have no way to know for certain if we are perceiving a material glass that is half full or a material glass is that half empty from our sense perceptions or if God is simply planting the idea of the glass and its contents in our mind."

Immanuel Kant (1724–1804)

"Although experience tells us that the glass is half empty, we must reason to believe that the glass is half full—to justify our moral code."

Johann Gottlieb Fichte (1762–1814)

"The glass and its contents are part of the universal ego."

Georg Wilhelm Friedrich Hegel (1770–1831)

"The mind develops a thesis that the glass if half full, then an antithesis that the glass is half empty, then unifies these opposites into a synthesis that the glass is neither half full nor half empty."

Johann Friedrich Herbart (1776–1841)

"The glass and its contents are merely the organization of 'reals.'"

John Stuart Mill (1806–1873)

"Through experience, the individual collects data, from which he draws conclusions, sometimes misusing this data to make subjective observations reflecting an optimistic or pessimistic bias."

Herbert Spencer (1820–1903)

"The glass is simultaneously half full and half empty."

William James (1842–1910)

"We have both the freedom and responsibility to see the glass as we please."

Friedrich Nietzsche (1844–1900)

"The glass is dead."

John Dewey (1859–1952)

"All we know for certain is that the glass contains something, but we must determine what that something is."

Jean-Paul Sartre (1905–1980)

"The question is absurd."

Albert Camus (1913–1960)

"It doesn't make any difference."

THINKERS AND STINKERS

WHO SAYS I KANT?

- German philosopher Immanuel Kant (1724–1804) was born, lived, and died in Königsberg, Prussia (known today as Kaliningrad, Russia). He never left Prussia and rarely left Königsberg.

- Baptized "Emanuel," Kant later changed the spelling of his first name to "Immanuel" to make it a more faithful rendering of the original Hebrew. Kant's mother nicknamed him "Manelchen," roughly meaning "little Manny."

- As a student, Kant spent most of his time playing pool.

- Legend holds that every afternoon, Kant took a walk at precisely 3:30 and was so punctual that local villagers would set their clocks by his appearance at his door.

- Legend holds that when Kant received a copy of *Émile* by Jean-Jacques Rousseau, he became so engrossed in the book that he neglected to take his customary afternoon walk.

- Kant never married, owned only one piece of art in his home, and ate only one meal a day—precisely at noon in the same restaurant—for sixty years.

- A university professor for most of his life, Kant did not achieve notoriety until he was in his late fifties.

- Both Ludwig van Beethoven and Johann Wolfgang von Goethe read Kant's writings.

Kant Condensed ➡️⬅️

Aside from insisting that the mind is actively involved in the objects it experiences, Kant's philosophy centers on his categorical imperative: "Always act in such a way that the maxim determining your conduct might well become a universal law." It's all a fancy way of saying it's okay for you to cheat, steal, and lie if you agree that it's okay for everyone in the world to cheat, steal, and lie.

WHAT KANT SAID

"There is . . . but one categorical imperative: 'Always act in such a way that the maxim determining your conduct might well become a universal law.'"

"Science is organized knowledge. Wisdom is organized life."

"Suicide is not abominable because God prohibits it; God prohibits it because it is abominable."

"The busier we are, the more acutely we feel that we live, the more conscious we are of life."

"I ought, therefore I can."

"He who is cruel to animals becomes hard also in his dealings with men. We can judge the heart of a man by his treatment of animals."

"Act so as to use humanity, in yourself or in others, always as an end and never as a means to an end."

"It is not necessary that while I live I live happily; but it is necessary that so long as I live I should live honorably."

"The science of mathematics presents the most brilliant example of how pure reason may successfully enlarge its domain without the aid of experience."

"God, freedom, and immortality are untenable in the light of pure reason."

"In law, a man is guilty when he violates the rights of another. In ethics, he is guilty if he only thinks of doing so."

"With men, the state of nature is not a state of peace, but war."

"Imagination is a powerful agent for creating, as it were, a second nature out of the material supplied to it by actual nature."

"Happiness is not an ideal of reason but of imagination."

"We are not rich by what we possess but by what we can do without."

JUST WHAT IS GOOD AND EVIL?

"The only good is knowledge and the only evil is ignorance."

—Socrates

"When choosing between two evils, I always like to try the one I've never tried before."

—Mae West

"Most of the evils of life arise from man's being unable to sit still in a room."

—Blaise Pascal

"The only thing necessary for the triumph of evil is for good men to do nothing."

—Edmund Burke

"To overcome evil with good is good, to resist evil by evil is evil."

—The Koran

"Non–cooperation with evil is as much a duty as is cooperation with good."

—Mahatma Gandhi

"Life is neither a good nor an evil; it is simply the place where good and evil exist."

—Lucius Annaeus Seneca

"We often do good in order that we may do evil with impunity."

—Duc de La Rochefoucauld

"Good judgment comes from experience. And where does experience come from? Experience comes from bad judgment."

—Mark Twain

"What is done out of love always takes place beyond good and evil."

—Friedrich Nietzsche

"The best of men cannot suspend their fate: The good die early, and the bad die late."

—Daniel Defoe

"Every sweet hath its sour; every evil its good."

—Ralph Waldo Emerson

"It's the good girls who keep diaries; the bad girls never have the time."

—Tallulah Bankhead

"What is moral is what you feel good after and what is immoral is what you feel bad after."

—Ernest Hemingway

"It is easier to denature plutonium than to denature the evil spirit of man."

—Albert Einstein

"Man is a being with free will; therefore, each man is potentially good or evil, and it's up to him and only him (through his reasoning mind) to decide which he wants to be."

—Ayn Rand

"I believe that unarmed truth and unconditional love will have the final word in reality. That is why right, temporarily defeated, is stronger than evil triumphant."

—Martin Luther King Jr.

"There are two types of people in this world, good and bad. The good sleep better, but the bad seem to enjoy the waking hours much more."

—Woody Allen

"Good girls go to heaven, bad girls go everywhere."

—Helen Gurley Brown

DOES GOD EXIST?

Is God a bearded old man sitting on a throne? Or is God an unknowable, indefinable, infinite force like in *Star Wars*? If God is everywhere, why would he want to be in the bathroom with me while I'm sitting on the toilet? Doesn't that make God an omniscient Peeping Tom? Or is God simply an organ grinder with man as his dancing monkey asking for small change?

The Ancient Jews (circa 1900 BCE)

One omniscient God is the creator and source of everything in the universe. And he says we get Saturdays off.

The Ancient Greeks (circa 1450–700 BCE)

A pantheon of immortal gods lived on Mt. Olympus in human form with human frailties. Led by Zeus, the gods had children with humans and each other. The major gods included Poseidon (god of the seas), Hades (god of the underworld), Aphrodite (goddess of beauty), Athena (goddess of wisdom), Hermes (messenger of the gods), Ares (god of war), and Apollo (god of light). And don't forget Dionysus, god of the intoxicating power of wine and the wild abandon that ensues.

Xenophanes (circa 570–475 BCE)

God is one, unseen and unchangeable, without a beginning or ending, effortlessly governing the universe. In fact, God is the universe, and the universe is God. God is everywhere, including your underwear drawer.

The Sophists (fifth century BCE)

The Greek belief in numerous gods is absurd, so people should conceive of the true God for themselves. And no cheating.

Socrates (469–399 BCE)

Socrates attempted to pioneer a clearer conception of God, but the citizens of Athens, convinced that he was subverting the popularly held belief in a pantheon of gods, condemned him to death. And that's why we worship Zeus to this very day.

Plato (circa 427–circa 347 BCE)

Possibly attempting to avoid the same fate as his teacher Socrates, Plato taught that a Demiurge, or divine architect, created the universe by using ideas to mold matter. The Demiurge created the gods of the Greek pantheon, but God created everything in the universe, including the soul of the world, and the souls of the planets. So Plato never really got his story straight.

Aristotle (384–322 BCE)

Forms are a force that realize themselves in matter, creating motion. Form moves matter, which, in turn, strives to be form—in a continuous cycle that culminates in pure form. This pure form is pure intelligence, the "unmoved mover," God—the cause of all motion, the unifying force that causes every being and object in the universe to strive for self-realization. In other words, God is an unseen personal trainer.

The Skeptics (circa fourth century BCE)

Man cannot possibly prove, reason, or intuit that God exists, so while God may exist, we must remain skeptical of that possibility. Of course, it doesn't hurt to sing God's praises, just in case.

The Epicureans (circa third century BCE)

Many gods—all with beautiful bodies of light shaped in human form—ate food, spoke the Greek language, had sex, and were oblivious to the world and mankind. Just like a typical fraternity toga party.

The Stoics (circa third century BCE)

One God is the soul of the world, resides in the outermost sphere of the universe, and from there pervades everything, giving life to the universe—and leaving it minty fresh.

Philo (circa 20–50 CE)

Attempting to show that Jewish beliefs about God were consistent with Greek philosophy, Philo taught that the one perfect and benevolent God is beyond man's comprehension, does not come into contact with matter, and his divine wisdom (an emanation from God called "Logos") created the world. God remains separate from the world, but fortunately, Pizza Hut delivers.

Plotinus (circa 205–270)

God, the unknowable source of everything in the universe, created the world through divine emanations. But now there's Beano.

St. Augustine (354–430)

God is eternal, omniscient, beneficent, and transcendent, the ultimate good-ness who created and controls the destiny of everything in the universe. The one God expresses himself in the universe as three emanations: God, Jesus Christ, and the Holy Spirit. It's the Trinity! Or three for the price of one!

John Scotus Erigena (circa 815–circa 877)

God and the universe are one, but the universe is only one small revelation of God, who is unknowable, benevolent, perfect, pure, wise, and busy working on a new project in some other dimension.

St. Anselm (1033–1109)

The idea that a perfect God exists proves that a perfect God does indeed exist. Yes, and the idea that a perfect woman exists proves that airbrushing exists.

Roscelin (circa 1045–1120)

The Trinity is three different divine beings with equal power. Like the Three Tenors—only better.

Peter Abelard (1079–1142)

The Trinity is made up of the Father (the power of God), the Holy Ghost (the good will of God), and the Logos (the wisdom of God). Exact ingredients may vary.

Richard of St. Victor (twelth century)

God cannot be understood through reason; instead, God can be understood only through a mystical ascension of the soul into the infinite truth, an out-of-body experience, a brief absorption of the self into God. Or a quickie in the supply closet.

Thomas Aquinas (circa 1225–1274)

Attempting to reconcile the teachings of Aristotle with Christian theology, Aquinas taught that God is pure form, an Unmoved Mover whose existence is implied by the observation that all of the movement in the universe must have a cause. God's existence is further proven by the ascending scale of existence, from the lowest forms of existence to the highest forms of existence, implying that at the top sits a perfect being. God is perfect, he is pure form, pure energy, the source of everything in the universe, who reveals himself through the universe—without having to flash open his trench coat.

Meister Eckhart (circa 1260–circa 1327)

All things are united through God, but God is incomprehensible to the human mind and can be known by man only through the Trinity, which continually flows in and out of God. God pervades all things, and all things pervade God, and ultimately we return to God—hopefully in first-class seats, not coach.

John Duns Scotus (circa 1265–circa 1308)

God, who is pure form or pure energy, has the infinite freedom to will or not will as he pleases, and consciously caused the universe for a purpose—which he refuses to tell anyone because he doesn't want to ruin the surprise ending.

Nicholas Cusa (1401–1464)

Man cannot use reason to know God, but through our intuition we can sense God. Or you can always try a Ouiji board.

Giordano Bruno (circa 1548–1600)

God pervades and sustains this infinite universe, unifying everything, beyond the grasp of the human mind. Kind of like Krazy Glue.

Jacob Boehme (1575–1624)

God is one, the source and union of everything in the universe. God created the universe through a blind yearning to become self–conscious of himself. So the world is one big group therapy session to help God get in touch with his feelings.

Francis Bacon (1561–1626)

We can obtain proof of God's existence through the study of nature, but we can attain knowledge of God's essence and divine law only through the church. Or by attending a Native American peyote ritual.

Thomas Hobbes (1588–1679)

God gave motion to everything in the universe and governs the world through the human rulers of the world. God may be a physical entity, but we can probably never truly know whether God is a Republican or Democrat.

René Descartes (1596–1650)

Since the idea of God—a perfect, omnipresent, omniscient, and infinite being—exists in Descartes' mind, that idea must have been planted by God, proving conclusively that God exists. God, the principal substance of the universe and independent of nature, created mind and matter, set the universe in motion, and preserves that motion. For Descartes, God is the "prime mover" of the universe. Kind of like that tattooed dwarf at the Round Meadow carnival who runs the Ferris wheel.

Blaise Pascal (1623–1662)

Man can come to know the pure spirit that is God only through spiritual or religious experience. Such as winning the lottery.

Benedict Spinoza (1632–1677)

God is the universe, the universe is God, and nothing exists independent of God, an infinite, eternal, self–initiated force that is the cause of every-thing. God is beyond human comprehension, and man can perceive only two aspects of God: thought (ideas) and extension (body). So keep your hands to yourself.

John Locke (1632–1704)

Man does not have an innate idea of God, but by gathering ideas from experience and extending them to infinity, man comes up with the notion of God—an all–knowing, just, and powerful spiritual substance that most definitely exists. God established divine laws, and man is rewarded or pun-ished in this world or the next world for how he adheres to these laws. And there's no plea bargaining.

Gottfried Wilhelm Leibniz (1646–1716)

The world is composed of independent monads with varying degrees of clarity, the clearest and most perfect being God, the cause of everything, who knows all and sees all. Man, made from less clear monads, cannot fully know God, made from perfectly clear monads. But man can get a sense of God by taking the good traits within himself and magnifying them to infinity. Magnifying your bad traits to infinity will give you, well, a peptic ulcer.

George Berkeley (1685–1753)

God, the source of everything in the universe, is pure consciousness. The world is an idea in God's mind and exists spiritually, not materially. So there's really no reason to mow the lawn, empty the trash, or do your laundry.

David Hume (1711–1776)

Since everything in the universe has a cause, the cause of the universe itself must be God, a perfect supreme being. God's existence cannot be proven, and humans are unqualified to adequately envisage God, who may very well be the soul of the universe—or quite possibly a bag lady living in an abandoned refrigerator box in downtown Pittsburgh.

Immanuel Kant (1724–1804)

The notion of God as the absolute oneness of everything is the supreme idea that man can have. This idea transcends experience, encompasses all experience, and can be obtained only through reason. Man turns this mighty idea into an entity and personifies it. Although it is impossible to prove the existence of God or comprehend him, man needs to believe in a perfectly wise and beneficent God who shares man's highest moral ideas—to justify developing an ethical code to live by. Otherwise, the world will go to hell in a hand basket.

Johann Gottlieb Fichte (1762–1814)

God, the source of the universe, is pure creative intelligence, "ego," a "universal life–force" ruling every individual's consciousness. The shared moral law instilled in every human being proves the existence of this universal ego called God. Yikes! It's contagious!

Friedrich Ernst Daniel Schleiermacher (1768–1834)

God and the world are one, and neither has ever existed without the other. However, God exists beyond space and time; the world exists in space and time. Man can know God, the creative intelligence of the universe and the source of everything, only through a spiritual sense of dependence. Or a clingy, self–destructive, manipulative, symbiotic relationship.

Georg Wilhelm Friedrich Hegel (1770–1831)

God is Idea, and through his creative reasoning process, the universe unfolds and evolves, enabling God to become self–conscious. And a little bit dizzy.

Auguste Comte (1798–1857)

All attempts to discover God are indicative of an immature mind, and instead, man must determine the relationships between phenomena. So buy yourself a tape measure, a stop watch, and a thermometer, and get to work.

Friedrich Wilhelm Joseph Schelling (1775–1854)

God is the soul and creative energy of the universe, which is alive. Oh no! Run for your lives!

Gustav Theodor Fechner (1801–1887)

God—the united psychic processes—is the soul of the world, and the world is the body of God. So sending a space probe to smash into a comet is like giving God a swift kick in the balls.

Søren Kierkegaard (1813–1855)

God is eternity, the infinite, the absolute, beyond human comprehension, and unavailable for lunch next Thursday.

Rudolf Hermann Lotze (1817–1881)

An absolute will unifies and expresses itself through all of the interrelated spiritual units that make up the world. And just wait till you get the monthly bill.

Herbert Spencer (1820–1903)

Man, confined to a finite existence, can know only that which is finite. Fully understanding the Infinite, then, is beyond man's grasp, making the unknowable truly unknowable. In other words, the great Herbert Spencer didn't have much of an imagination compared to a Swiss patent office examiner named Albert Einstein.

William James (1842–1910)

Although we cannot prove whether God exists or accurately define God, man has a need to believe in a God who pervades the universe and helps man fulfill his ethical and moral principals. Or at least helps him find the car keys.

Jean-Paul Sartre (1905–1980)

There is no God, and even if God did exist, it wouldn't make any difference because man is free to design his own meaning and purpose in life, free from any influence from God. So if God does exist, he's not paying attention anyway.

"God is dead."

Friedrich Nietzsche's proclamation that "God is dead" is one of philosophy's most misunderstood and misinterpreted quotations. Nietzsche did not mean that divine power does not exist. He meant that religion had lost its relevance and could no longer serve as the foundation for moral values. He urged people to re-evaluate and reconstruct their value systems. Nietzsche proclaimed "God is dead" in his book *Thus Spake Zarathustra*, published in 1885. Eleven years later in 1896, German composer Richard Strauss composed his tone poem *Thus Spake Zarathustra* as a homage to Nietzsche, attempting to convey through music the development of the human race from its origin to Nietzsche's idea of the Overman, the highly evolved individual who has mastered self-control over his animal instincts and rechannels those passions through creativity. In 1969, director Stanley Kubrick used the beginning of Strauss' *Thus Spake Zarathustra* to accompany the opening sequence of his landmark film *2001—A Space Odyssey*, which visually depicts the development of the human race. Still, if Nietzsche believed that life is pointless, why did he write so many books?

OH YEAH?
PROVE GOD EXISTS!

Impossible, you say? Fear not. Most philosophers agree that there's no way to rationally demonstrate that God exists, which means there's no shortage of irrational ways to make an utterly illogical case that God sits on high, whatever that means. Here are the top three arguments for the existence of God, none of which proves diddly squat—but all of which confirm that you, like scores of renowned philosophers from the past, can make a total fool of yourself.

The Cosmological Argument

THE ARGUMENT: The universe exists, so someone or something must have created it.

THE LOGICAL FLAW: If God created the universe, who created God? And who created God's creator? Ad infinitum.

The Ontological Argument

THE ARGUMENT: In the eleventh century CE, St. Anselm of Canterbury argued that God is the most perfect being imaginable. If God is perfect, he must have all perfections, including existence. If God lacks existence, he is not perfect. Since God is perfect, he must exist.

THE LOGICAL FLAW: Perfection does not necessarily include existence.

The Teleological Argument

THE ARGUMENT: The universe is intricately ordered, intelligently designed, and seems to be acting according to a divine plan for a purpose.

THE LOGICAL FLAW: There is also a great deal of chaos in the universe, and science reveals that all phenomena in the universe has a logical or random cause. Ascribing a purpose to the existence of the entire universe as a whole is subjective.

THE WORLD'S GREATEST PHILOSOPHERS

Plato

Starting in 1978, child actress Dana Plato played Kimberly Drummond on the hit television sitcom *Diff'rent Strokes,* starring Gary Coleman. In 1984, the producers fired Plato from the show when she became pregnant, although after she gave birth to a son, she made several cameo appearances on the show. After the series, Plato posed in *Playboy,* became addicted to cocaine, starred in several pornographic films (including one titled *Different Strokes*), and was arrested for robbing a video store in Las Vegas with a pellet gun in 1991. When she was arrested the following year for forging a prescription for Valium, singer Wayne Newton bailed her out in the hopes of helping her turn her life around. In 1999, Plato died from an overdose from Loritab and Vicodin. Her death was ruled a suicide. Plato's enduring philosophy? "I'm okay in my skin, you know . . . I'm okay with who I am."

Aristotle

In 1923, a year after Turkey recaptured Smyrna from Greece, Aristotle Onassis moved to Argentina, revived his family's tobacco business, and in 1925, became a dual citizen. During the decade that followed, Onassis purchased some commercial ships and soon became the first Greek ship-owner to enter the tanker business. In 1946, he married Athina Livanos, the daughter of Greek shipping magnate Stavros Livanos, and later became the brother-in-law of Stavros Niarchos, another powerful Greek shipping magnate. In 1957, he founded Olympic Airways, the Greek national airlines. After having a notorious affair with opera diva Maria Callas, Onassis divorced his first wife in 1961, and later ended his relationship with Callas to marry Jacqueline Bouvier Kennedy, the widow of slain President John F. Kennedy, in 1968. Onassis best summed up his philosophy of life: "If women didn't exist, all the money in the world would have no meaning."

Hobbes

A character in the comic strip *Calvin and Hobbes* by cartoonist Bill Watterson, Hobbes is a stuffed animal that belongs to the child Calvin, who sees Hobbes as a living, breathing tiger. Other characters in the comic strip perceive Hobbes as a lifeless stuffed animal. Named after British philosopher Thomas Hobbes, Hobbes plays and talks with Calvin, frequently pounces him playfully (inflicting genuine injuries), loves tuna fish, and makes sardonic comments about human nature. Does Calvin merely imagine that Hobbes is alive, or does the stuffed animal come to life only when Calvin is alone? Explains Watterson in the *Tenth Anniversary Book:* "Hobbes is more about the subjective nature of reality than dolls coming to life."

Berkeley

A director and choreographer of movie musicals, Busby Berkeley began his choreography career while serving as an artillery lieutenant in the United States Army during World War I, when he was ordered to stage a parade in France. Soon after, he organized several stage shows for the soldiers. After the war, Berkeley staged extravagant dance numbers for the Broadway musical *Holka–Polka*, became one of Broadway's top dance directors, and was called to Hollywood in 1930 by Samuel Goldwyn. He became famous for his elaborate dance routines featuring scores of showgirls and for his overhead camera shots in the films *Palmy Days, Roman Scandals, Gold Diggers of 1933, 42nd Street*, and *Gold Diggers of 1935*. Berkeley later directed *Strike Up the Band, For Me and My Gal, The Gang's All Here, Cinderella Jones*, and *Take Me Out to the Ball Game*, and on Broadway he directed *No, No Nanette*. Declared Berkeley philosophically: "I wanted to make people happy, if only for an hour."

Hume

Best known for his role in the movie *Cocoon*, Hume Cronyn was married for fifty-two years to actress Jessica Tandy, with whom he co-starred on Broadway in *The Gin Game* and *Foxfire*. Hume starred in the movies *Phantom of the Opera, Lifeboat, The Postman Always Rings Twice, People Will Talk, Cleopatra, There Was a Crooked Man, The World According to Garp*, and *Brewster's Millions*. In 1944, he was nominated for an Academy Award for Best Supporting Actor for his role in *The Seventh Cross*. He won two Tony Awards: in 1964, as Best Supporting Actor for playing Polonius in Shakespeare's *Hamlet*, and, in 1994, receiving a Lifetime Achievement Award shared with his wife. Hume adhered to one philosophy as an actor: "If you're doing the devil, look for the angel in him. If you're doing the angel, look for the devil in him."

Marx

Born Julius Henry Marx in 1890, Groucho Marx was best known as the wise-cracking leader of the Marx Brothers, with a trademark cigar, wire-rimmed glasses, and a thick, black, greasepaint mustache and eyebrows. His insulting one–liners, delivered with leering eyes, were often non-sequiturs laced with sexual innuendo. In the Marx Brothers movies, he played a womanizing swindler with a heart of gold and an uncanny name, such as Rufus T. Firefly, Hugo Z. Hackenbush, and Otis B. Driftwood. After the Marx Brothers stopped making movies, Groucho hosted the hit television game show *You Bet Your Life*. His philosophy? "I don't want to belong to any club that will accept me as a member."

James

Grammy Award–winning funk entertainer Rick James achieved international stardom in 1981 with his album "Street Songs," which included the hit songs "Super Freak," "Give It to Me Baby," and "Fire and Desire." In 1993, James, addicted to cocaine, was convicted of assaulting two women. He served two years in Folsom Prison. His philosophy can be best summed up by the lyrics to his mega-hit song "Super Freak," in which he strongly urges that you don't take a girl who's pretty kinky home to meet your mother.

Dewey

Having served for three terms as governor of New York, Thomas Dewey was nominated twice as the Republican candidate for President of the United States, in 1944 and 1948. Predicted by pollsters as the inevitable winner of the 1948 presidential election, Dewey's name was immortalized by a famous photograph of presidential winner Harry S. Truman holding up a copy of a St. Louis newspaper with an incorrect headline reading "Dewey Defeats Truman." Convinced that he had an unsurpassable lead in polls, Dewey had waged a noncommittal campaign to avoid offending any voters. Philosophized Dewey: "When you're leading, don't talk."

THINKERS AND STINKERS

WHAT'S HAPPENING
WITH HOBBES

- British philosopher Thomas Hobbes (1588–1679) translated Thucydides' *History of the Peloponnesian War* from Greek into English, the first time the book was ever translated into English.

- Hobbes translated both Homer's *Iliad* and *Odyssey* into English.

- Hobbes served as secretary to Sir Francis Bacon, tutored William Cavenish (who later became Earl of Devonshire), and while in Italy, befriended Galileo Galilei.

- While living in Holland, Hobbes tutored mathematics to Charles, the Prince of Wales, who later was crowned King Charles II and forbade the publishing of Hobbes' work.

- Hobbes was afraid to sleep in the dark.

- In his book *Leviathan*, Hobbes claims that geometry "is the only science that it hath pleased God hitherto to bestow upon mankind."

- In *Leviathan,* Hobbes states, "Do not that to another, which thou wouldst not have done to thyself," convinced that his maxim marks the first time anyone has ever stated the converse of the Golden Rule espoused by Jesus in the New Testament. However, the Jewish rabbinic sage Hillel said the same thing as Hobbes sixteen centuries earlier.

- Nearly every major philosopher disagrees with Hobbes, who claimed that all human action is ultimately based upon selfishness, with no sense of morality or social responsibility. Hobbes also insisted that man is a purely selfish creature who must be restrained by the strong hand of authority.

- Cartoonist Bill Watterson named the tiger in his comic strip *Calvin and Hobbes* after Thomas Hobbes.

- At the age of eighty-four, Hobbes wrote his autobiography—in Latin verse.

- Hobbes died at the age of ninety-one.

Hobbes Condensed ➡◀

Convinced that everything in the universe is matter in motion and subject to the laws of cause and effect, Hobbes argued that man must discover the laws of motion in order to comprehend the universe and put these laws to work for his benefit. It also pays to learn CPR and the Heimlich maneuver.

WHAT HOBBES SAID

"Truth and False are attributes of speech, not of things. And where speech is not, there is neither Truth nor Falsehood."

"The Papacy is not other than the Ghost of the deceased Roman Empire, sitting crowned upon the grave thereof."

"The secret thoughts of a man run over all things, holy, profane, clean, obscene, grave and light, without shame or blame."

"Sometimes justice cannot be had without money."

"Such is the nature of men, that howsoever they may acknowledge many others to be more witty, or more eloquent, or more learned; yet they will hardly believe there be many so wise as themselves."

"The world is governed by opinion."

"Words are . . . the money of fools."

CAN GOD MAKE A ROCK SO BIG THAT EVEN HE CAN'T LIFT IT?

Xenophanes (circa 570–475 BCE)

"God is the rock, and the rock is God."

Socrates (469–399 BCE)

"A rock unexamined is not worth lifting."

Plato (circa 427–circa 347 BCE)

"The Demiurge molds God's idea of the rock into matter, and God has no interest in lifting it."

Aristotle (384–322 BCE)

"God, the pure intelligence of the universe, the 'unmoved mover,' shapes matter into a large rock and causes the rock to strive for self-realization."

Philo (circa 20 circa–circa 50 CE)
"Logos, an emanation from God, creates a large rock, but God refuses to come into contact with matter and instead remains separate from the world."

St. Augustine (354–430)
"God can create and control the destiny of the rock."

John Scotus Erigena (circa 815–circa 877)
"God and the rock are one, so the rock is unknowable."

St. Anselm (1033–1109)
"The very idea that God can make a rock so big that even he can't lift it proves that God can indeed make a rock so big that even he can't lift it."

Richard of St. Victor (twelfth century)
"Man cannot fathom the existence of such a rock through reason, but only by becoming one with God."

Thomas Aquinas (circa 1225–1274)
"God, being pure form and perfect, can definitely make a rock so big that he can't lift it, but man, being imperfect, cannot comprehend how this can be so."

Meister Eckhart (circa 1260–circa 1327)
"God pervades the rock, the rock pervades God, and ultimately the rock returns to God."

John Duns Scotus (circa 1265–circa 1308)
"God can do as he pleases."

Giordano Bruno (circa 1548–1600)

"God surely has the ability to make a rock so big that he can't lift it, but God's abilities are beyond the grasp of the human mind."

Francis Bacon (1561–1626)

"Only through the church can we come to sense whether God can make a rock so large that even he cannot lift it."

Jacob Boehme (1575–1624)

"God can create the rock to become self–conscious of itself."

Thomas Hobbes (1588–1679)

"God may be a able to fashion a rock so grand that even he cannot lift it, but we can probably never truly know for certain."

René Descartes (1596–1650)

"The idea of a rock so large that even God cannot lift it exists in the mind of man. That idea was obviously placed in man's mind by God, proving that God—the prime lifter—can indeed make a rock so large that even he can't lift it."

Benedict Spinoza (1632–1677)

"God is the rock, the rock is God, and nothing can be lifted independent of God, the cause of all lifting."

John Locke (1632–1704)

"Man's idea of the rock—a body so large that God cannot lift it—most definitely exists."

Gottfried Wilhelm Leibniz (1646–1716)

"The rock is composed of monads that are dull, whereas God is composed of perfectly clear monads."

George Berkeley (1685–1753)

"The rock is an idea in God's mind and exists spiritually, not materially."

David Hume (1711–1776)

"God can cause a rock to exist and he can cause a rock not to be lifted, but we cannot prove God's existence, thus we cannot prove the existence of such a rock."

Immanuel Kant (1724–1804)

"The idea that God can create a rock so large that even he cannot lift it transcends experience, exceeds man's comprehension, and cannot be proved one way or the other. Man, however, needs to believe that God can create a rock so large that even he cannot lift it—to reconcile his conception of God as all powerful."

Johann Gottlieb Fichte (1762–1814)

"The universal ego is not concerned with proving its capabilities to man."

Friedrich Ernst Daniel Schleiermacher (1768–1834)

"God does not exist without the rock, and the rock does not exist without God."

Georg Wilhelm Friedrich Hegel (1770–1831)

"By melding thesis with antithesis, God can impose form on matter to create a rock so large that he cannot lift it, and this synthesis further enriches God's self–consciousness."

Auguste Comte (1798–1857)

"The question reflects the idiosyncrasies of an undeveloped mind."

Rudolf Hermann Lotze (1817–1881)

"The absolute will can create anything it wishes, even a rock so large that it cannot be lifted."

Herbert Spencer (1820–1903)

"Man's finite existence prevents him from ever knowing whether the Absolute would even care to create a rock so large that it cannot be lifted."

William James (1842–1910)

"We cannot prove that God exists, and if he does exist, we cannot prove that he is capable or incapable of making a rock so large that even he cannot lift it."

Friedrich Nietzsche (1844–1900)

"God is dead, so the answer is no."

Jean-Paul Sartre (1905–1980)

"What God?"

Albert Camus (1913–1960)

"The question seems to demand an answer, but I can't really be sure if I understand the question, and I don't see how it is of any consequence any way, since I doubt that anyone will be satisfied with any answer I might give."

WHAT THEY SAID
ABOUT GOD

"And the day will come when the mystical generation of Jesus by the Supreme Being, in the womb of a virgin, will be classed with the fable of the generation of Minerva in the brain of Jupiter."

—Thomas Jefferson

"The idea of God is the sole wrong for which I cannot forgive mankind."

—Marquis de Sade

"I do not believe in the divinity of Christ, and there are many other of the postulates of the orthodox creed to which I cannot subscribe."

—William Howard Taft

"This is all that I've known for certain, that God is love. Even if I have been mistaken on this or that point: God is nevertheless love."

—Søren Kierkegaard

"Religion is all bunk."

—Thomas Edison

"Religion is comparable to a childhood neurosis."

—Sigmund Freud

"When I think of all the harm the Bible has done, I despair of ever writing anything to equal it."

—Oscar Wilde

"The most beautiful system of the sun, planets, and comets, could only proceed from the counsel and dominion on an intelligent and powerful Being."

—Sir Isaac Newton

"We have just enough religion to make us hate, but not enough to make us love one another."

—Jonathan Swift

"Man is a marvelous curiosity . . . he thinks he is the Creator's pet . . . he even believes the Creator loves him; has a passion for him; sits up nights to admire him; yes and watch over him and keep him out of trouble. He prays to him and thinks He listens. Isn't it a quaint idea?"

—Mark Twain

"The beauty of the world and the orderly arrangement of everything celestial makes us confess that there is an excellent and eternal nature, which ought to be worshiped and admired by all mankind."

—Marcus Tullius Cicero

"Religion is regarded by the common people as true, by the wise as false, and by rulers as useful."

—Lucius Annaeus Seneca

"The divinity of Jesus is made a convenient cover for absurdity."

—John Adams

"The Christian religion not only was at first attended with miracles, but even at this day cannot be believed by any reasonable person without one."

—David Hume

"At present there is not a single credible established religion in the world."

—George Bernard Shaw

"It is easier to suppose that the universe has existed for all eternity than to conceive a being beyond its limits capable of creating it."

—Percy Bysshe Shelley

"Is man merely a mistake of God's? Or God merely a mistake of man?"

—Friedrich Nietzsche

"To believe in God is impossible—not to believe in Him is absurd."

—Voltaire

"Even God cannot change the past."

—Agathon

"It is fear that first brought gods into the world."

—Petronius

"Mathematics is the language in which God wrote the universe."

—Galileo Galilei

"To regard Christ as God, and to pray to him, are to my mind the greatest possible sacrilege."

—Leo Tolstoy

"I believe in God, only I spell it Nature."

—Frank Lloyd Wright

"By simple common sense I don't believe in God, in none."

—Charlie Chaplin

"I don't believe in God as I don't believe in Mother Goose."

—Clarence Darrow

"I don't believe in God. My god is patriotism. Teach a man to be a good citizen and you have solved the problem of life."

—Andrew Carnegie

"The Bible is not my book nor Christianity my profession. I could never give assent to the long, complicated statements of Christian dogma."

—Abraham Lincoln

"I don't believe in God, so I'm not afraid of dying."

—B. F. Skinner

"All thinking men are atheists."

—Ernest Hemingway

"How much reverence can you have for a Supreme Being who finds it necessary to include such phenomena as phlegm and tooth decay in His divine system of Creation? What in the world was running through that warped, evil, scatological mind of His when He robbed old people of the power to control their bowel movements?"

—Joseph Heller

"An agnostic is somebody who doesn't believe in something until there is evidence for it, so I'm agnostic."

—Carl Sagan

"God is a concept by which we measure our pain."

—John Lennon

"If you want to get together in any exclusive situation and have people love you, fine—but to hang all this desperate sociology on the idea of The Cloud–Guy who has The Big Book, who knows if you've been bad or good—and *cares* about any of it—to hang it all on that, folks, is the chimpanzee part of the brain working."

—Frank Zappa

"We must question the story logic of having an all–knowing all–powerful God, who creates faulty Humans, and then blames them for his own mistakes."

—Gene Roddenberry

"Religion has convinced people that there's an invisible man . . . living in the sky. Who watches everything you do every minute of every day. And the invisible man has a list of ten specific things he doesn't want you to do. And if you do any of these things, he will send you to a special place, of burning and fire and smoke and torture and anguish for you to live forever, and suffer, and burn, and scream, until the end of time. But he loves you. He loves you. He loves you and he needs money."

—George Carlin

"If the average man is made in God's image, then such a man as Beethoven or Aristotle is plainly superior to God."

—H.L. Mencken

"It may be that our role on this planet is not to worship God—but to create him."

—Arthur C. Clarke

"What thinking man is there who still requires the hypothesis of a God?"

—Friedrich Nietzsche

"The Force is what gives the Jedi his power. It's an energy field created by all living things. It surrounds us and penetrates us. It binds the galaxy together."

—Alec Guinness in *Star Wars*, 1977

WHAT WERE THEY THINKING?

FATE VS. FREE WILL

Are we all just marionettes on strings operated by God? Are we mere pawns in a cosmic chess game? Or can you leap off that chess board and become the thimble in a game of Monopoly? Most philosophers through the ages have said man is free as a fart in a windstorm, but many others have said that each one of us is nothing but a tile on a cosmic Scrabble board, unaware that we've been used to spell the word *quim* and score triple letter points. Well, actually no philosopher ever said that, but here's what they have said:

The Ancient Greeks (circa 1450–700 BCE)
The Fates, powers of the universe, control man's destiny. Although there also seems to be a lot of dumb luck involved.

Pythagoras (580–500 BCE)
The nature of the universe determines man's fate, but by understanding numbers, man can unlock the secrets of fate—and possibly master Sudoku.

Heraclitus (circa 535–circa 475 BCE)

The world operates eternally according to unalterable cosmic law, and man is subject to his fate and must accept it as inevitable. Particularly if he gets stuck in an elevator.

The Sophists (fifth century BCE)

Man is not completely a prisoner of fate and has the ability to shape his own destiny within society. Unless he gets blackballed.

Socrates (469–399 BCE)

By attaining knowledge, man acquires the ability and freedom to shape his destiny—and obtain a lower interest rate on a home mortgage.

Plato (circa 427–circa 347 BCE)

Man has the choice whether to act justly and wisely according to reason or to surrender to his base desires. In other words, man has the free will to live a good, just life, or put a lampshade on his head and dance the Hoochie Coochie.

Aristotle (384–322 BCE)

Man is free to do good (realizing his full potential to be all that he can be) or to do evil (and have one helluva time).

Epicurus (circa 342–270 BCE)

Man is composed of atoms that have the power to freely move as they will, giving man the inner power to freely act as he wills. So the atoms that comprise your body give you the freedom to order a pizza with any topping your atoms desire.

Zeno the Stoic (circa 336–264 BCE)

Everything in the universe, including man's will, adheres to fixed and unalterable laws, and the very nature of the world unleashed a never–ending chain reaction of causes and effects that result in predetermined events and actions. Man is merely a cog in a wheel, free only to accept his fate happily or unhappily. I'll drink to that!

The Stoics (circa third century BCE)

Everything in the world has evolved and continues to evolve to fulfill God's purpose. But man is free to decide whether he will conquer his animal desires, abide by moral law, and take the 7:20 commuter train into work.

Philo (circa 20 circa–circa 50 CE)

Attempting to reconcile Jewish beliefs with Greek philosophy, Philo taught that the soul, endowed with the spark of divine intelligence, but trapped in a body, has the power to choose between surrendering to bodily desires or mastering them and elevating himself to seek the divine within himself. Or just take two aspirins and call me in the morning.

Plotinus (circa 205–270)

Man's soul is a part of the world soul, but imprisoned by the body, man's soul is free to embrace the sins of the body or to strive to reunite with God, who is perfect freedom. Either way, bring your video camera.

The Apologists (circa third century)

At the creation, some souls, given the freedom to choose between good and evil, chose God and other souls turned from God and embraced the sins of matter by taking bodies. God sent Jesus to earth to enable those sinful souls to redeem themselves, if they so choose. Otherwise, those poor souls do not pass Go and do not collect $200.

St. Augustine (354–430)

The first man, Adam, had free will, but when he chose to sin, he ended free will for all mankind for eternity and his sin became hereditary. All men are born with original sin, but God has predetermined whom he will save and who will endure eternal damnation. And that's non–negotiable.

Peter Abelard (1079–1142)

Man is free to choose between good and evil, because only through choice can sin exist. And without sin, the Catholic church would go out of business.

Thomas Aquinas (circa 1225–1274)

Man, endowed with both intelligence and a will, uses his intelligence to determine his actions, and can use his will to act in the interest of the higher good. Still, man inherited original sin from Adam, but when God offers man salvation, man is free to choose if he wishes to accept it. Or he can have an all-expenses-paid trip to the fiery inferno of the Hotel Lucifer.

John Duns Scotus (circa 1265–circa 1308)

The human will is perfectly free to arbitrarily choose between good and evil, based on information provided by the human intellect. Unfortunately, the human intellect generally works on a sixth-grade reading level.

Francis Bacon (1561–1626)

Man must free himself from the shackles of past beliefs and study the universe objectively, but man, subject to the will of God, must obey religious laws even if they seem unreasonable. So man is free as long as he doesn't leave his jail cell.

Thomas Hobbes (1588–1679)

Everything in the universe, including the actions and fate of man, is subject to the laws of cause and effect. This mechanized world causes opposing desires and aversions within man, who deliberates until he reaches the final desire or aversion, which is his will (his decision to act or not act) and is clearly predetermined. So you're essentially nothing more than an elaborate pre-programmed computer with a belly button.

René Descartes (1596–1650)

The body is subject to a predetermined mechanical process based on the laws of cause and effect, but the soul is free to choose to work for the higher good and direct the body's actions. Likewise, the soul is free to chose to work at the Department of Motor Vehicles for the rest of your life.

Benedict Spinoza (1632–1677)

God is self–caused, self–determined, and totally free, but God has set everything in the universe into motion on a predetermined course, a successive chain of events. For Spinoza, there is no free will. A man's will is simply his mind affirming an idea as true or false, and this affirmation is predetermined by the idea itself. Man, unaware of this sequence of predetermined causes and effects, sees himself as free. The same way Calista Flockhart sees herself as voluptuous, Paris Hilton sees herself as down-to-earth, and Donald Trump sees himself as sophisticated.

John Locke (1632–1704)

Every individual has the power to decide how he wishes to act upon his thoughts and every man has the power to take action, so therefore man clearly possesses the free will to choose between Ashley and Mary-Kate.

Gottfried Wilhelm Leibniz (1646–1716)

Everything in the world is composed of independent, insulated, self-determined monads. Man, composed of an intricate combination of monads, is free from outside influence and freely determines his dreams and desires according to his own nature. Man freely chooses his strongest desire, based on what his nature tells him is best, and his will strives to attain it—explaining why some people just can't stop squeezing the Charmin.

David Hume (1711–1776)

Just as there is cause and effect in nature, there is this same necessity for cause and effect in human behavior in that desires cause actions. However, as long as man's actions result from his character, he is free. But if his actions result from a bottle of whiskey on a Saturday night, he has to pay child support.

Jean-Jacques Rousseau (1712–1778)

Man is not a machine whose thoughts and actions are predetermined by the natural laws of cause and effect. Instead, man is a feeling, sensitive creature with a free soul who strives to balance freedom and responsibility. Except when he's behind the wheel of a car during rush hour.

Immanuel Kant (1724–1804)

Although experience shows us that the laws of cause and effect suggest that we live in a mechanical, predetermined world with no free will, reason enables us to transcend experience and conceptualize the idea of free will. Even though there is no way to prove that free will exists, man must believe in free will to hold himself and other people responsible for their actions, to strive to live a moral life, and to feel a sense of accomplishment when taking out the trash.

Johann Gottlieb Fichte (1762–1814)

The ego of each individual is independent of the natural laws of cause and effect because each individual ego is a part of the Absolute ego of the universe, which is free, creative, and self-determined. We are free to decide whether we will serve the Absolute ego willingly or unwillingly. Get with the program, sourpuss.

Friedrich Ernst Daniel Schleiermacher (1768–1834)

Each individual ego is a part of the Absolute and must conform to the laws of the universe, but each individual ego is also bestowed with unique skills and talents that it must develop to help enable the Absolute to fully realize itself. Oh Lordy, pick a bale of cotton! Oh Lordy, pick a bale of hay!

Georg Wilhelm Friedrich Hegel (1770–1831)

For God to become fully self-conscious, man must become fully self–conscious, and man can only become fully self-conscious if he is free to realize the nature of the universe and hence himself to the fullest. This may also require several cups of espresso and an ice cold shower.

Friedrich Wilhelm Joseph Schelling (1775–1854)

Man is an expression of God, the soul and creative energy of the living universe, which is free. Free at last! Free at last! Thank God Almighty, we're free at last!

Johann Friedrich Herbart (1776–1841)

Just as everything in the universe follows fixed laws of science, man follows strict laws of human behavior, and therefore man has no free will—but impeccable table manners.

Arthur Schopenhauer (1788–1860)

The guiding principal of the universe is will, a constant, eternal striving that can be found in everything. In man, this will is self-conscious and capable of having pity and sympathy for others, sacrificing his own self–interests, and negating his own will—proving that man has free will. Or that a sucker is born every minute.

John Stuart Mill (1806–1873)

Although human behavior can be frequently predicted, behavior is determined by many factors, including the desire of the individual. This desire allows the individual to decide upon a course of action worthy of praise or blame, proving that man has free will. Either that, or a martyr complex.

Thomas Hill Green (1836–1882)

Man's ability to picture a better world enables him to strive to achieve those ideas, improving himself and his environment, fully responsible for his actions. Thus, man has the free will to better his existence. Or lead the country into yet another quagmire.

William James (1842–1910)

Man has a will to believe whatever system of philosophy that satisfies his reason, and this will to believe illustrates that man is free to believe whatever set of ideals he chooses. Even if it involves a bushel of Ping Pong balls and a pair of ice tongs.

Friedrich Nietzsche (1844–1900)

All human behavior is motivated by "the will to power"—the desire of people to gain self-control over their own animal instincts. Nietzsche's idealized *Übermensch*, or Overman, is the person who can control passions and rechannel them through creativity—such as sublimating your sex drive and using that repressed energy to build a gothic cathedral.

John Dewey (1859–1952)

Man is a creative part of the unfolding universe, free to make decisions that advance the evolution of the world—like whether to wallpaper the bathroom.

Jean-Paul Sartre (1905–1980)

Man is condemned to be free, but this freedom provides the ultimate opportunity for man to give meaning to his life and fill the world with meaning, achieving his existential authenticity and becoming editor of the high school yearbook.

No Metamorphosis

Czechoslovakian writer Franz Kafka portrayed a world ruled by despair, alienation, existential angst, and oppression from anonymous forces beyond anyone's control. In his classic short story "The Metamorphosis," insurance salesman Gregor Samsa awakes to discover that he has turned into a giant insect. But what if Gregor had woken up to an entirely different reality?

Gregor Samsa awoke one morning from a good night's rest. He laid on his back, beneath the blankets, his head resting on the pillow. He could still hear the cacophonous ringing that had jarred him from his sleep. On the table beside his bed, a small hammer pounded furiously at two small golden bells on an alarm clock, and the key mechanism in the back unwound rapidly. "How about if I go back to sleep and forget all this nonsense?" thought Gregor; and he reached to turn off the alarm and then buried his head beneath the blankets once more.

But it was impossible to go back to sleep this morning; there was something frightfully wrong. Gregor turned back the coverlet, sat himself up, and rolled his legs over the side of the bed until they touched the floor. His hands grasped the curve of the mattress.

"Egad!" he thought, and he stretched out his arms, extending his fingers as he yawned. His fingers slowly became fists and pulled inward, returning his hands to his shoulders and then to his knees. He felt a little itch behind his neck, and reached back with his left hand to scratch the spot. There were no pitiably thin legs fluttering helplessly before his eyes; there were no pains in his stomach; no brownish liquid oozed from his mouth, although his tongue felt a bit stale and there was a crusty feeling about his eyes. Gregor stretched again and looked over into the mirror sitting on the night table beside his clock.

"Gaaa!" he exclaimed at the sight of his reflection. "I must be dreaming!" He rubbed the sleep from his eyes, and then he pinched himself to see if he was still asleep. But much to his dismay, he discovered that he was wide awake. He looked back at the alarm clock ticking on the table. It was half-past seven; there was still plenty of time to make the train to work by nine. He fell back down on the bed, exhausted by the thought. "It is only seven-thirty," he reflected. He listened to the sound of the clock ticking, as though, by waiting a few moments on the bed he would change into something besides his normal self. However, the clock soon read seven forty-five and he still had no excuse for missing work that morning. He could call in sick, he thought, but his parents would never be a party to deceit. He would have to get up and get dressed.

Gregor rose from his bed and walked over to his bureau. He opened the drawers and found his clothes. At the breakfast table he would have time to devote proper attention to resolve his trouble. After dressing himself, he turned the key effortlessly to open the door from his room. He walked down the hallway without any trouble and entered the kitchen. He stood nervously behind his chair at the table, hoping his appearance would not startle his family. Gregor's father did not raise his head from his morning paper. His mother turned from the stove, her hair in curlers, skillet in hand. "Good morning, dear," she said. His father lifted his head from his paper and added, "Sit down and have some breakfast." But Gregor was overcome with terror and rushed off, slamming the door behind him.

"I wonder what has gotten into him," his mother was heard to say.

There had to be some reason for this madness, Gregor thought. He walked quickly down the street, wrapping himself in his jacket, wearing dark glasses, a hat on his head with the brim pulled down, and covering his face with a handkerchief so no one would take notice.

People turned their heads to stare. "Why do they look at me like that?" Gregor thought. "Why can't they mind their own business?" The people wondered why such a nice young man would hide his face so. "Perhaps he is a criminal," they thought, and soon a police officer was following Gregor down the street.

Gregor did not know what to think. "Oh, how simple life would be if I had woken up this morning as a cockroach," Gregor thought. The police officer was still following him.

Gregor started walking at a faster pace down the street, but the police officer was hot on his tail, though Gregor did not actually have one this morning. He signaled for a cab. "Take me straight to the City Police Headquarters!" he exclaimed in an anguished voice.

He ran up the steps of the hall and entered the building. "May I see the District Inspector?" he asked a man at the front desk.

"What can I do for you?" asked the District Inspector.

"The whole thing is just too ridiculous for words," Gregor said.

"Maybe if you'd take the handkerchief from your face and take off those dark glasses, I could help you with whatever seems to be wrong," said the Inspector.

"But don't you see?" Gregor asked, still holding the handkerchief in front of his face. "That's just the problem! Nothing is wrong!"

"Nothing is wrong?" snapped the Inspector. "What do you mean by interrupting police business if nothing is wrong?"

"I can't quite explain it," explained Gregor. "But now I shall have to go to work and support my family. Don't you see?"

"I can't see anything with that handkerchief in front of your face," snapped the Inspector.

"How can you joke in a matter like this?" asked Gregor angrily.

"There he is! Don't move!" came a shout from across the room. Gregor looked up to see the police officer who had been chasing him earlier. The officer was holding up his gun with both hands and pointing the nose of the firearm directly at Gregor. "Put up your arms," he shouted.

"Who me?" Gregor asked.

The police officer forced Gregor to spread his arms and legs against the wall so the Inspector could frisk him.

"This guy's been acting awfully suspicious," said the officer.

"Yes," agreed the Inspector, "he has been sort of buggy."

"I have?" Gregor asked, hopefully.

Gregor was placed in a small prison cell. He sat on the bunk bed, staring at the wall. "At least now I will not have to go to work," he thought. The plaster was chipping off the wall before him, and as Gregor let his eyes wander along the crack, he noticed a small beetle crawling up the wall. "What I wouldn't give to be in his shoes," Gregor mused.

In the dark courtroom, five wooden chairs sat along a gray wall. Gregor and his Defense Attorney sat in two of these. A terribly serious judge sat at the bench and began to rustle solemnly through a file of papers for a few minutes as if to emphasize the gravity of Gregor's case. At frequent intervals he would raise his eyebrows as he came upon some particularly interesting tidbit of information amidst the wealth of papers. "Hmmmm," he would mutter to feign intrigue.

Finally, he turned to Gregor and said, "Tell me all you know about this incident."

Gregor stood and told the Judge all he knew, which was nothing.

The Prosecutor then rose. "Why were you walking down the street trying to cover your face?" he asked Gregor.

"I wasn't feeling myself," Gregor replied. "I didn't want anyone to notice."

"To notice what?"

"That nothing had happened."

"When a police officer began to follow you, you hopped into a taxi," said the Prosecutor. "Why did you flee?"

"I didn't notice anyone following me," said Gregor. "I was much too upset to notice things."

"Much too upset with what?"

"My condition," insisted Gregor.

"And what condition was that?" asked the Prosecutor.

"My lack of any condition," said Gregor.

"Could you be more specific?"

Gregor remained uncertain as to what crime he had been accused of. "I'm in no condition to describe my condition."

"Under what condition would you be willing to tell us?" asked the judge.

"Your honor, the horrible truth is that I just can't live in these conditions without having a condition."

"Why did you go to police headquarters to report a crime that hadn't been committed?"

"Because nothing had happened," confessed Gregor.

"Your honor," said the Prosecutor, addressing the judge, "I accuse the prisoner of behaving this morning in a way that clearly showed he was guilty of a crime. This lowly man is nothing but an insect, a parasite of society."

"I am?" thought Gregor, touching his face to feel if he suddenly had mandibles and antennae. But all he felt was the stubble on his unshaven face.

"We the people demand that justice be served, that he be adequately punished for his crime, that no harm should ever come to the public. It is our civic duty."

"Guilty!" said the judge, banging his gavel.

Gregor pictured himself sitting in a jail cell forever, free from his stifling family, free from his job at the insecticide factory, free from society and all its demands and trappings. From now on he would be a free man in his prison cell.

The judge banged the gavel again. "The prisoner shall rise," said the judge. Gregor rose to his feet and stood at attention. "Mr. Samsa, you are hereby sentenced to death," said the judge.

The room began to spin, and the next thing Gregor knew, he was strapped to a wooden chair and gas was filling the room. He felt a strange queasiness in his stomach and was suddenly overcome by fatigue, his eyelids growing heavy. Today turned out much differently than I anticipated, thought Gregor, as he slipped into unconsciousness, never to spread his wings again.

THINKERS AND STINKERS

DESPERATELY SEEKING DESCARTES

- When French philosopher René Descartes (1596–1650) was one year old, his mother died. So Descartes, along with his brother, Pierre, and his sister Jeanne, were raised by their grandmother.

- In 1633, Descartes finished writing the manuscript for a book titled *Le Monde* (The World), but upon hearing that the Church had condemned Galileo Galilei that same year for insisting that the earth revolved around the sun, Descartes decided against publishing his book for fear that he too would be condemned by the Church. Like Galileo, Descartes had assumed Nicolaus Copernicus' theory that the earth revolved around the sun.

- Descartes never married, but in 1635, one of his domestic servants, Helene, gave birth to a baby girl, named Francine. According to a baptismal record, the father was Descartes.

- Descartes invented analytic geometry, was the first philosopher to describe the physical universe in terms of matter and motion, and initiated the attempt to formulate universal laws of motion.

- In his essay "Geometry," Descartes showed how certain geometrical problems can be solved using algebraic equations, paving the way for Sir Isaac Newton to develop calculus.

- Contrary to popular belief, Descartes did not develop the "Cartesian Coordinate System" that bears his name, or the "Cartesian Product."

- Descartes stood 5 foot 1 inch tall, wore a wig, and slept in the nude.

- Descartes died in Sweden. Since he was a Catholic, and Sweden was a Protestant country, he was buried in Adolf Fredriks kyrkogård, a cemetery in Stockholm reserved for unbaptized children. In 1667, his remains were taken to Paris and buried in the Church of St. Genevieve–du–Mont. During the French Revolution, his remains were disinterred for burial in the Pantheon in Paris among the great French thinkers. His tomb is now in the church of St. Germain-des-Pres. The French treasurer general, who supervised the move of the body, kept the bones from Descartes' right hand as a personal souvenir. Descartes' skull is preserved in the Musée de l'Homme in Paris, France.

Descartes Condensed ▶◀

Dubbed a dualist, Descartes believed the world is composed of two basic substances: matter (the physical universe) and spirit (intelligence). One should be washed in warm water, the other in cold water with your fine washables .

WHAT DESCARTES SAID

"I think, therefore I am."

"It is not enough to have a good mind. The main thing is to use it well."

"The greatest minds are capable of the greatest vices as well as the greatest virtues."

"One cannot conceive anything so strange and so implausible that it has not already been said by one philosopher or another."

"Common sense is the most widely shared commodity in the world, for every man is convinced that he is well supplied with it."

"In order to improve the mind, we ought less to learn than to contemplate."

"The reading of all good books is like conversation with the finest men of the past centuries."

"When it is not in our power to determine what is true, we ought to follow what is most probable."

"If you would be a real seeker after truth, it is necessary that at least once in your life you doubt, as far as possible, all things."

"The chief cause of human errors is to be found in the prejudices picked up in childhood."

PHILOSOPHIES
THAT FAILED

Aristotle's Blunders

Greek philosopher Aristotle (384–322 BCE) incorrectly insisted that the earth was the center of the universe and that the sun rotated around the earth. These preposterous ideas were accepted as fact for nearly two-thousand years and embraced by the Vatican, resulting in the persecution of several great scientific minds, most notably Italian astronomers Giodano Bruno (circa 1548–1600) and Galileo Galilei (1564–1642).

Aristotle also incorrectly claimed that:

- A heavier body falls faster than a lighter body.

- A body falls at a speed in proportion to its weight (meaning a ten-pound weight falls ten times faster than a one-pound weight).

- The space between the moon and the earth is full of air.

- The human embryo is produced solely from the sperm.

- Sound is carried to our ears by the movement of air. (Sound travels in waves.)

Anaximenes the Airhead

The sixth century Greek philosopher Anaximenes of Miletus believed that air was the basic substance of the universe, and everything else stems from air through rarefaction or condensation.

Sour Atoms

The Greek natural philosopher Democritus (circa 460–370 BCE) first proposed the theory that all matter is composed of atoms. However, he also incorrectly theorized that atoms could not be split, that atoms were solid, that sour tastes were caused by sharp atoms, and that the human soul was made up of the smallest atoms in the universe.

All You Need Is Love

Greek philosopher Empedocles (circa 495–435 BCE) incorrectly claimed that everything in the universe is composed of four elements (earth, air, fire, and water), which he insisted were bonded together by love and driven apart by strife.

For the Love of Leibniz

German philosopher Gottfried Wilhelm Leibniz (1646–1716) insisted in his book *Théodicée*, published in 1710, that everything is for best in this, the best of all possible worlds, because the universe was created by God. Leibniz's philosophy came crashing down in 1755, when an earthquake in Lisbon, Portugal, killed some 60,000 people, including many people who died in the rubble of the churches where they had been observing All Saints Day. French writer Voltaire lambasted Leibniz's philosophy in his book *Candide*, caricaturing Leibniz's adherents through the character Dr. Pangloss, an absurdly overzealous optimist.

Everybody Needs Somebody

Swiss doctor, alchemist, and philosopher Theophrastus Phillippus Aureolus Bombastus von Hohenheim (1493–1541), better known as Paracelsus, believed that a human being has two bodies: a visible body that belongs to the earth, and an invisible body (attuned to imagination and spiritual aspects) that belongs to heaven.

Plato and the Hiccups

The ancient Greek philosopher Plato (circa 428–circa 348 BCE) insisted that the cure for hiccups was to gargle while holding your breath.

The Posidonius Adventure

The ancient Greek philosopher Posidonius (circa 135–31 BCE) inaccurately estimated the circumference of the earth to be 18,000 miles. The circumference of the earth is 24,901.55 miles at the equator and 24,859.82 miles through the poles.

WHY DID THE CHICKEN CROSS THE ROAD?

Heraclitus (circa 535–circa 475 BCE)
"To abide by the laws of nature."

Protagoras (fifth century BCE)
"To determine its own fate."

Socrates (469–399 BCE)
"A road unexamined is not worth crossing."

Plato (circa 427–circa 347 BCE)
"To dwell in the realm of ideas."

Aristotle (384–322 BCE)
"To take part in the divinity of the universe."

St. Augustine (354–430)
"To return to God."

Thomas Aquinas (circa 1225–1274)

"To seek redemption and be reunited with God."

Francis Bacon (1561–1626)

"To free itself from the shackles of conventional beliefs."

Thomas Hobbes (1588–1679)

"It was subject to the laws of cause and effect."

René Descartes (1596–1650)

"To remain in harmony with the laws of cause and effect."

Benedict Spinoza (1632–1677)

"Because God set everything in the universe into motion on a predetermined course."

John Locke (1632–1704)

"Because it decided to do so."

Gottfried Wilhelm Leibniz (1646–1716)

"A central monad controlling the intricate combination of monads that make up the chicken gave the chicken the will to cross the road."

George Berkeley (1685–1753)

"Because God planted the idea in the mind of the chicken."

David Hume (1711–1776)

"We cannot be certain that the chicken and the road physically exist, but if they do, the chicken desired to cross the road."

Immanuel Kant (1724–1804)

"The chicken embraced the moral truths within itself and took control of its own destiny, crossing the road."

Johann Gottlieb Fichte (1762–1814)

"Because the chicken is an expression of the Absolute ego of the universe."

Friederich Ernst Daniel Schleiermacher (1768–1834)

"To help the universe reach its full creative potential."

Georg Wilhelm Friedrich Hegel (1770–1831)

"Because a thought in the chicken's brain evolved from thesis to antithesis to synthesis."

Johann Friedrich Herbart (1776–1841)

"Because the 'reals' that comprise the chicken's brain interacted according to fixed laws of nature."

Auguste Comte (1798–1857)

"We can never understand the inner essence of the chicken."

John Stuart Mill (1806–1873)

"Far too many factors must be considered to accurately determine why the chicken takes any course of action."

Herbert Spencer (1820–1903)

"To continue evolving along with the universe."

William James (1842–1910)

"For whatever reason you wish to believe."

Friedrich Nietzsche (1844–1900)

"It was driven by the will to power."

John Dewey (1859–1952)

"To advance the evolution of the world."

Bertrand Russell (1872–1970)

"Because, ruled by the vast mathematical machine that governs the world according to scientific laws, the chicken had no choice but to follow its predetermined fate."

Martin Heidegger (1889–1976)

"To reach its ontological oneness–as–such."

Jean–Paul Sartre (1905–1980)

"The chicken is absurd."

Albert Camus (1913–1960)

"It is of no consequence."

TAKING SPINOZA FOR A SPIN

- Born to a Jewish family in Amsterdam and given an orthodox Jewish upbringing and education, Baruch Spinoza (1632–1677) became one of the most famous Jews to ever be excommunicated from the Jewish community. The rabbis of Amsterdam expelled him at the age of twenty-four for denying the existence of angels, the immortality of the soul, and the divine authorship of the Torah. Spinoza immediately changed his first name from the Hebrew Baruch (meaning "Blessed") to the Latin form of the name, Benedict.

- Spinoza earned a living by grinding and polishing lenses for eyeglasses, telescopes, and microscopes.

- Offered a professorship of philosophy at Heidelberg University, Spinoza turned down the opportunity so that he could philosophize unencumbered by academic responsibilities.

- Spinoza's most popular book, *Ethics,* was published after his death.

- Spinoza was working on a translation of the Hebrew Bible into Dutch when he died.

- Spinoza died from a problem with his lungs, believed to have been caused by inhaling powdered glass during the many years that he worked grinding lenses.

- Another famous Jew, Albert Einstein, when asked if he believed in God, replied, "I believe in Spinoza's God who reveals himself in the orderly harmony of all that exists, not in a God who concerns himself with fates and actions of human beings."

- In the 1950s, Israeli Prime Minister David Ben–Gurion urged the rabbis of Amsterdam to withdraw Spinoza's excommunication. The rabbis did not take any action.

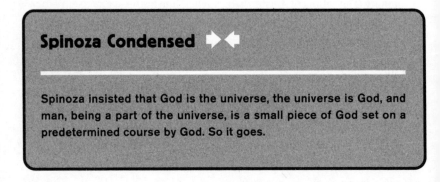

Spinoza Condensed ➤◄

Spinoza insisted that God is the universe, the universe is God, and man, being a part of the universe, is a small piece of God set on a predetermined course by God. So it goes.

WHAT SPINOZA SAID

"He who would distinguish the true from the false must have an adequate idea of what is true and false."

"The more we understand individual things, the more we understand God."

"Peace is not an absence of war, it is a virtue, a state of mind, a disposition for benevolence, confidence, justice."

"I would warn you that I do not attribute to nature either beauty or deformity, order or confusion. Only in relation to our imagination can things be called beautiful or ugly, well–ordered or confused."

"I have made a ceaseless effort not to ridicule, not to bewail, not to scorn human actions, but to understand."

"If you want the present to be different from the past, study the past."

"Nature abhors a vacuum."

"Will and intellect are one and the same thing."

"Men govern nothing with more difficulty than their tongues."

"A vain man may become proud and imagine himself pleasing to all when he is in reality a universal nuisance."

"Fear cannot be without hope nor hope without fear."

"Those who are believed to be the most abject and humble are usually the most ambitious and envious."

"Avarice, ambition, lust, etc., are nothing but species of madness."

THE SOUL AND DEATH

What is the soul? A divine spark? A lithium battery? Or a figment of the human imagination? Does the soul truly exist? And if so, where does the soul go after death? To the Bahamas? Rio de Janeiro? Siberia? Does the soul reunite with God? Burn in hell? Or does it get reincarnated into a new body that can eat as much as it wants without ever gaining an ounce? Or does the soul die with the body, never to be heard from again—even if it reverses the charges?

Anaximenes of Miletus (sixth century BCE)

The soul is thin air that holds the body together. Upon death, the soul leaves the body, which then disintegrates. Yep, into thin air.

Pythagoras (580–500 BCE)

How a person lives in this life determines the fate of the soul after death. So finish everything on your plate.

Heraclitus (circa 535–circa 475 BCE)

Souls, made from a fine form of fire, vary in quality, cannot be destroyed, and occasionally set off the smoke alarm in the family room.

Empedocles (495–435 BCE)

Upon death, the soul leaves the body and transmigrates to another body—ideally one that doesn't already have a soul.

Democritus (460–370 BCE)

The soul, responsible for reason, is made of the purest fire atoms scattered throughout the body, and upon death these indestructible fire atoms leave the body and scatter throughout the universe and rearrange themselves to create another being—possibly the Human Torch.

Plato (circa 427–circa 347 BCE)

A Demiurge created the universe and gave it an immortal world soul, endowed the planets with immortal souls, and bestowed each individual with an immortal soul. The human soul strives to return to the realm of pure ideas, where it existed before it was given a body. Upon death of the body, the soul either returns to its star of origin forever or it transmigrates into another body. Fortunately for Plato, electroshock therapy was not introduced until 1938.

Aristotle (384–322 BCE)

All living things have souls with varying degrees of sophistication, but man, having the power to reason creatively, sits at the top of this ladder. Man's creative reason is an immortal spark of God, which upon death of the body, returns to God. And if it's more than three days overdue, you have to pay a late fee.

Epicurus (circa 342–270 BCE)

The soul, composed of fine atoms of fire, air, breath, and infinitesimal specs of matter, is scattered throughout the body and is controlled by a rational part located in the chest. When the body dies, the soul atoms scatter throughout the universe, and the soul no longer exists. Like pixie dust.

The Stoics (circa third century BCE)

The soul is a spark of the divine fire, controlled from somewhere near the heart. Just like the pilot light on a gas stove.

Plotinus (circa 205–270)

The human soul is part of the world soul that chose to mold itself into matter and now struggles to free itself from matter. Upon the death of the body, the human soul, being immortal, either succeeds in its quest to return to God and achieves self–realization, or it fails and transmigrates into another human body, animal, plant, or ventriloquist dummy.

St. Augustine (354–430)

The soul, which is spiritual, directs the actions of the body, which is material. The soul, though not an emanation from God, is immortal, and depending whether the individual lives a righteous life, after death the soul is either blessed for eternity in a realm of bliss or condemned to a realm of eternal damnation—much like the Greyhound bus station in Schenectady, New York.

Thomas Aquinas (circa 1225–1274)

God creates the human soul at birth, and after the death of the body, this intellectual soul lives on in spiritual form for eternity. Possibly in a safety deposit box.

Ludovico Vives (1492–1540)

Man must undertake precise scientific study of the soul to determine how it works. But it's highly unlikely that your health insurance will cover any of this.

Bernardino Telesio (1509–1588)

Humans have two souls: a material soul, composed of a fine heat–like substance that resides in the brain and controls the body through the nervous system, and an immortal soul added by God. So it's buy one, get one free.

Francis Bacon (1561–1626)

Man has two souls: one rational (to be understood by religion), the other irrational (to be understood by science). Or think of one soul as peanut butter and the other as chocolate.

Thomas Hobbes (1588–1679)

The entire world is material, therefore, an immaterial soul does not exist whatsoever—making it even more difficult to find your soul mate.

René Descartes (1596–1650)

The soul, immaterial and distinct from the body, is a part of God and expresses itself through willing, feeling, and reasoning. After the death of the body, the soul continues to exist, completely unaffected. It gets helplessly lost and ends up at a bachelor party in Soho.

Benedict Spinoza (1632–1677)

The soul is a mode of God, subject only to spiritual laws and free from the laws of science. After the death of the body, the soul remains immortal as a mode of God—and can sneak into movie theaters without having to buy a ticket.

John Locke (1632–1704)

The soul is a purely immaterial thing that thinks, perceives, and wills. The soul can influence and move bodies, and bodies can influence the soul. We can have faith that the soul is immortal, but we cannot prove it through reason. So just in case it's not, see the Grand Canyon *before* you die.

Gottfried Wilhelm Leibniz (1646–1716)

Just as the world is composed of an infinite number of independent monads with varying degrees of clarity, humans contain a "queen monad" or soul that unifies and harmoniously guides all of the monads that make up the human body. The soul monad, possessing innate knowledge, moves toward self–realization. All monads are eternal, and when the body dies, the monads disperse and live on—as does the soul monad, which takes a long, well–needed vacation, probably in the Caribbean.

George Berkeley (1685–1753)

The world is an idea in God's mind and exists spiritually, not physically. Man's soul is a creation of God, and as such, is an eternal part of the spiritual essence of the world, now available in three great scents—apple cinnamon, mountain spring, and new outdoor fresh.

David Hume (1711–1776)

We cannot know for certain if the soul exists, or if it does exist, if the soul is immortal. All we can know for certain is that we experience a succession of perceptions. By the way, this soup is cold.

Immanuel Kant (1724–1804)

Although man cannot experience the soul, man can reason that the soul is the true essence of his combined mental processes. Believing in the existence of the soul and its immortality is valuable because it allows us to give one unifying name to the many aspects of our spiritual nature and sense of identity. The idea of the soul also helps us to live ethical lives, enabling us to meet the demands of the moral law. It also gives us something valuable to sell to the devil.

Johann Gottlieb Fichte (1762–1814)

The universal ego, the absolute creative principal of the universe, is broken up into the individual egos that reside in each person. These immortal individual egos are instilled with the moral law and remain connected to the universal ego—although the reception can sometimes be fuzzy.

Friedrich Ernst Daniel Schleiermacher (1768–1834)

Each individual ego, while a part of the Absolute ego, is independent and instilled with a unique skill or talent that it must realize and develop to contribute to the evolution of the Absolute. Like fashion design, party planning, or shuffle board.

Johann Friedrich Herbart (1776–1841)

The world is composed of unalterable "reals" that combine to form objects, and the soul is a real in the brain. When the body dies and the reals that compose the body disperse, the soul, like all reals, continues to exist. Well, in Herbart's vivid imagination anyway.

Arthur Schopenhauer (1788–1860)

Each individual possesses an immortal will that is part of the universal will, to which it returns upon death of the body. Like they say, you can take the boy out of Brooklyn, but you can't take Brooklyn out of the boy.

Auguste Comte (1798–1857)

The search for a soul and belief in its immortality reflect a nascent stage of man's intellectual development and must be discarded into the festering garbage heap of putrid ignorance.

Rudolf Hermann Lotze (1817–1881)

The soul resides in the brain and controls the body. Although no one knows for certain what happens to the soul after death, Lotze has faith that the soul receives a just reward or punishment for its deeds on earth. So like your mom said, always use the magic words.

William James (1842–1910)

The belief in a soul and its immortality may serve a useful purpose for those striving to lead a moral life, but the belief has no basis in reality. But hey, if a placebo cures your hay fever, keep taking it.

Friedrich Nietzsche (1844–1900)

There is no heaven or hell; instead people relive their lives over and over in the exact same way for all eternity. Through his insistence upon this concept of "eternal recurrence," Nietzsche hoped to provoke people to accept and love life so completely and passionately that they would choose to relive it forever. Or die trying.

John Dewey (1859–1952)

Belief in a soul and its immortality prevents man from seeking a deeper scientific understanding of experience. Although laziness may also be a major factor.

PHILOSOPHY KILLS

Anaxagoras (circa 500–397 BCE)

Sentenced to death for claiming that the sun was a red hot stone rather than a god, but ultimately exiled instead.

Aristotle (384–322 BCE)

Accused of impiety for his philosophic views by the Athenians and exiled to Chalcis, where he died.

Francis Bacon (1516–1626)

Imprisoned in the Tower of London for bribery.

Giordano Bruno (circa 1548–1600)

Imprisoned by the Inquisition in Italy for insisting that the universe is infinite and burned alive at the stake.

Tommaso Campanella (1568–1639)

Persecuted by the Inquisition and imprisoned for twenty-seven years for agreeing with Copernicus' view that the earth revolves around the sun.

Albert Camus (1913–1960)

Killed in a car accident at the age of forty-six.

Marcus Tullius Cicero (106–43 BCE)

Murdered by emissaries of Mark Antony for opposing the Second Triumvirate's rule of Rome.

John Amos Comenius (1592–1670)

Persecuted by Polish partisans who burned his house and manuscripts in Moravia, forcing him to flee to Amsterdam.

Galileo Galilei (1564–1642)

Condemned to death by the Inquisition, but escaped the sentence by agreeing not to teach that the earth revolves around the sun.

David Hume (1711–1776)

Persecuted in Switzerland and France for sedition and impiety.

Hypatia (370–415)

Beaten to death by Christian monks, who burned her remains.

Le Mettrie (1709–1751)

Persecuted and believed to have been poisoned.

Niccolò Machiavelli (1469–1527)

Arrested, tortured, imprisoned, and exiled by the Medici family, who ruled Florence.

Friedrich Nietzsche (1844–1900)

Suffered a nervous breakdown, spent a year in a sanitarium, and was cared for by his mother and sister until his death.

Pelagius (circa 360–circa 420 CE)

Condemned by Pope Zosimus and banished from Rome.

Protagoras (fifth century BCE)

Banished from Athens for his agnosticism, and while escaping, died in a shipwreck.

Jean–Paul Sartre (1905–1980)

Captured by the Nazis while serving in the French Army and held as a prisoner of war for nine months.

Socrates (469–399 BCE)

Condemned to death by a jury of two thousand people for expressing views considered subversive and forced to drink a cup of hemlock.

Benedict Spinoza (1632–1677)

Excommunicated from the Jewish community of Amsterdam for his philosophic views.

Miguel de Unamuno y Juga (1864–1936)

Fired as rector of the University of Salamanca and expelled from Spain for criticizing the king and dictator.

Voltaire (1694–1778)

Imprisoned several times for his satirical writings.

HANGIN' WITH HUME

- Scottish philosopher David Hume (1711–1776) was sent by his family to attend the University of Edinburgh at the age of twelve.

- As a student at the University of Edinburgh, Hume told a friend, "there is nothing to be learned from a professor, which is not to be met with in books."

- Hume's most influential and important work, *A Treatise of Human Nature,* written when he was age twenty–six, failed to provoke a public reaction in Great Britain upon its initial publication. According to Hume, the book "fell dead–born from the press, without reaching such distinction as even to excite a murmur among the zealots."

- In 1744, after the publication of his second book, *Essays Moral and Political,* Hume applied for the chair of Ethics and Pneumatics at Edinburgh University but was rejected. Four years later, he applied for the chair of Philosophy at the University of Glasgow and was rejected again.

- Hume wrote *The History of Great Britain* in six volumes, which became a bestseller.

- Around 1770, Hume achieved notoriety after German philosopher Immanuel Kant extolled his work and acknowledged that it had awoken him from "dogmatic slumbers."

- Because the British government frequently sentenced critics of Christianity to death for blasphemy, Hume did not acknowledge authorship of *A Treatise of Human Nature* until the year of his death, in 1776, and his essays *Of Suicide, Of the Immortality of the Soul,* and *Dialogues Concerning Natural Religion* were not published until after his death— and even then without acknowledging the names of the author or publisher.

Hume Condensed ➤◀

Arguing that people constantly make erroneous scientific and philosophic generalizations based on a few isolated cases, Hume believed that just because one event always precedes a second event doesn't prove that the first event caused the second event. The young woman may be slapping the young man's face for some reason other than his promiscuous advances.

WHAT HUME SAID

"Beauty in things exists in the mind which contemplates them."

"History is the discovering of the constant and universal principles of human nature."

"Truth springs from argument amongst friends."

"He is happy whose circumstances suit his temper; but he is more excellent who can suit his temper to any circumstances."

"The sweetest path of life leads through the avenues of learning, and whoever can open up the way for another, ought, so far, to be esteemed a benefactor to mankind."

"Nothing can be more unphilosophical than to be positive or dogmatical on any subject."

"Reason is the slave of the passions."

WHERE IS THE SOUL LOCATED?

Hippocrates (circa 460–circa 377 BCE)
In the brain

Plato (circa 427–circa 347 BCE)
In the brain, which, together with the spinal cord, coordinates this vital force

Aristotle (384–322 BCE)
In the heart

Strato (circa 340–circa 270 BCE)
In the front of the brain, between the eyebrows

Herophilus (335–280 BCE)
In the calamus scriptorius, the reed–like part of the rhomboid fossa of the fourth ventricle of the brain

Erasistratos (circa 304–250 BCE)

In the cerebellum

Galen (129–200)

In the fourth ventricle of the brain

Hippolytus (circa 180–circa 230)

Near the pineal gland

St. Augustine (354–430)

In the middle ventricle of the brain

Roger Bacon (circa 1214–1294)

In the center of the brain

Mondino de Liuzzi (1275–1326)

In the third ventricle of the brain

Ludovico Vives (1492–1540)

In both the heart (the center of its physical activity) and the brain (the center of its intellectual activity)

René Descartes (1596–1650)

In the pineal gland

Herbert Spencer (1820–1903)

In the pons cerebri

Michael Servetus (1511–1553)

In the Aqueduct of Sylvius, the channel connecting the third and fourth ventricle of the brain

Andreas Vesalius (1514–1564)

In the brain

Raymond Vieussens (1641–1715)

In the centrum ovale

Emanuel Swedenborg (1688–1772)

In the corpora striata, a pair of large ganglia of the brain

THINKERS AND STINKERS

BEWARE OF VOLTAIRE

- French philosopher François Marie Arouet (1694–1778) went by the pen–name Voltaire, a name he adopted while in prison.

- After his graduation from the Collège Louis–le–Grand in Paris, Arouet decided to become a writer, against the wishes of his father, who wanted him to become a lawyer. Pretending to work as a lawyer's assistant, Arouet spent most of his time writing poetry. Eventually, his father discovered the truth and sent him to the provinces to study law, but Arouet continued writing.

- In 1717, one of Arouet's satirical writings about Philippe II, the Duke of Orléans, got him arrested and imprisoned in the Bastille for eleven months.

- While in prison, Voltaire adopted the pen name and wrote his first play, *Oedipe,* which became a theatrical success.

- In 1726, Voltaire insulted the Chevalier de Rohan and, given the choice between imprisonment or exile, fled to England, where he was influenced by the works of William Shakespeare, John Locke, and Sir Isaac Newton.

- After three years of exile in England, Voltaire returned to France and published his ideas in a fictional book entitled *Philosophical Letters on the English*, praising English customs and culture. The French monarchy, interpreting the book as an attack, ordered copies of the book to be burned, and Voltaire fled Paris again.

- In 1749, Voltaire moved to Potsdam, Germany, where his new benefactor, Frederick the Great, gave him an annual salary of 20,000 francs—until Voltaire angered him by publishing *The Diatribe of Doctor Akakia*, an attack on the president of the Berlin Academy of Science. Frederick ordered that all copies of the book be burned and had Voltaire arrested.

- Voltaire never said, "I disagree with what you say but will defend to the death your right to say it." This saying was written by E. Beatrice Hall, in her 1907 book, *Friends of Voltaire*, as a paraphrase of a quote from his *Essay on Tolerance*, "Think for yourselves and let others enjoy the privilege to do so too." The closest Voltaire came to the quote was in a letter to the Abbe A.M. DeRiche in 1770: "I detest what you write, but I would give my life to make it possible for you to continue to write."

- Voltaire is credited for having said, "If God did not exist, it would be necessary to invent him." But Archbishop John Tillotson of Canterbury (1630–1694) said the same thing in a sermon long before Voltaire was born ("If God were not necessary a Being in Himself, He might almost seem to be made for the use and benefit of men"), who was similarly preceded by the Roman poet Ovid (43 BCE–17 CE) ("It is convenient that there be gods, and, as it's convenient, let us believe there are").

- When Voltaire died in Paris at the age of eighty-three, he was denied burial in church ground because of his criticism of the church. His heart and brain were removed from his dead body before it was embalmed and buried at the abbey of Scellieres in Champagne, France. His heart, preserved in a silver case, was given to his niece and lover Madame Denis, who later bestowed it to hotelier Madame de Villette. On July 10, 1791, Voltaire's remains were moved to the Pantheon in Paris. In 1814, a group of right–wing religious zealots secretly stole Voltaire's remains and dumped them in a garbage heap. No one noticed that Voltaire's sarcophagus was empty until 1864, when it was opened to place the heart inside. Today, Voltaire's preserved brain is in the Bibliotheque Nationale in Paris. For more than one hundred years, a series of private custodianships possessed Voltaire's heart, but the heart mysteriously disappeared after an auction.

Voltaire Condensed ▶◀

A firm believer in God, Voltaire condemned all dogmatic religions as intolerant and superstitious, particularly those that persecuted him.

WHAT VOLTAIRE SAID

"Those who can make you believe absurdities can make you commit atrocities."

"Animals have these advantages over man: They never hear the clock strike, they die without any idea of death, they have no theologians to instruct them, their last moments are not disturbed by unwelcome and unpleasant ceremonies, their funerals cost them nothing, and no one starts lawsuits over their wills."

"The superfluous, a very necessary thing."

"Tears are the silent language of grief."

"Appreciation is a wonderful thing; it makes what is excellent in others belong to us as well."

"The best way to be boring is to leave nothing out."

"It is not enough to conquer; one must learn to seduce."

"It is forbidden to kill; therefore all murderers are punished unless they kill in large numbers and to the sound of trumpets."

"We have a natural right to make use of our pens as of our tongues, at our peril, risk, and hazard."

"I envy animals for two things—their ignorance of evil to come, and their ignorance of what is said about them."

"God is a comedian playing to an audience too afraid to laugh."

"It is said that God is always on the side of the heaviest battalions."

"In general, the art of government consists of taking as much money as possible from one class of citizens to give to another."

"History is but the record of crimes and misfortunes."

"Judge a man by his questions rather than his answers."

"Illusion is the first of all pleasures."

"Is there anyone so wise as to learn by the experience of others?"

"Liberty of thought is the life of the soul."

"Love is a canvas furnished by Nature and embroidered by imagination."

"Love truth, but pardon error."

"Marriage is the only adventure open to the cowardly."

"Minds differ still more than faces."

"There are no sects in geometry."

"The infinitely small have a pride infinitely great."

"The individual who prosecutes a man, his brother, because he is not of the same opinion, is a monster."

"The biggest reward for a thing well done is to have done it."

"This agglomeration which was called and which still calls itself the Holy Roman Empire was neither holy, nor Roman, nor an empire."

"The sentiment of justice is so natural, and so universally acquired by all mankind, that it seems to be independent of all law, all party, all religion."

"Think for yourselves and let others enjoy the privilege to do so, too."

"Men use thought only to justify their wrong doings, and employ speech only to conceal their thoughts."

"It is dangerous to be right in matters on which the established authorities are wrong."

"Not to be occupied, and not to exist, amount to the same thing."

"It is better to risk saving a guilty person than to condemn an innocent one."

" . . . it would be very singular that all nature, all the planets, should obey eternal laws, and that there should be a little animal five feet high, who, in contempt of these laws, could act as he pleased, solely according to his caprice."

"Common sense is not so common."

"Doubt is not a pleasant condition but certainty is an absurd one."

"I have never made but one prayer to God, a very short one: 'O Lord, make my enemies ridiculous.' And God granted it."

"Man is free at the moment he wishes to be."

"Doctors prescribe medicine of which they know little, to cure diseases of which they know less, in human beings of which they know nothing."

"I know of nothing more laughable than a doctor who does not die of old age."

"The art of medicine consists of amusing the patient while nature cures the disease."

"It is an infantile superstition of the human spirit that virginity would be thought a virtue and not the barrier that separates ignorance from knowledge."

"Tyrants have always some slight shade of virtue; they support the laws before destroying them."

"Optimism, said Candide, is a mania for maintaining that all is well when things are going badly."

"Anything that is too stupid to be spoken is sung."

"To succeed in the world it is not enough to be stupid, you must also be well–mannered."

"No problem can withstand the assault of sustained thinking."

"A witty saying proves nothing."

"He who thinks himself wise—O heavens!—is a great fool."

TAKE THE NESTEA PLUNGE

American philosopher Henry David Thoreau (1817–1862) adamantly believed in the "unquestionable ability of man to elevate his life by conscious endeavor," but what if Thoreau, who sequestered himself at his isolated house on Walden Pond in Massachusetts, had ruminated on something as simple as a glass of iced tea?

Living in the solitude of Walden Pond and having ample time to contemplate the intricacies of the human condition with a glass of iced tea in my hands, I came to meditate upon the precept that most men in this relatively free country, imprisoned by blind obedience to the struggles of day-to-day existence, fail to take a moment to reflect upon the simple pleasures of life, like sipping the very glass of iced tea I held in my hands. The mass of men, living in quiet desperation, slaving to earn a living, know what quenches the thirst, not what quenches the spirit. To the wise man, that majority of one living in solitude, leisurely sipping a glass of iced tea becomes an act of self–emancipation—a conscious endeavor to deliberately elevate the soul, to delve into life, to take, if you will, the Nestea plunge.

By the words, *Nestea plunge*, I mean to convey more than the simple idea that sipping a tall glass of iced tea on a hot summer day refreshes the body like a plunge into my Walden Pond for a brisk swim in the winter months. Rather, the Nestea plunge is the humble tonic of contemplation that rejuvenates the mind, catapulting one into a more reflective state from whence the soul can be free and unconstrained. Surely, it is imperative that we drink iced tea to the beat of a different drummer. Otherwise, we do not drink iced tea, it drinks us. For that reason, I urge any visitor who chances by my house on Walden Pond—nay, I beseech them—to take the Nestea plunge! Of course, this also helps deplete my supply of the dehydrated tea, affording me an impeachable excuse to go into the village to purchase more jars of the mix and temporarily escape the insufferable seclusion that has driven me to seek meaning in something as innocuous as a glass of iced tea. I sorely need a new gimmick.

GRAVE ISSUES:
WHERE ARE THE GREAT PHILOSOPHERS OF ALL TIME BURIED?

Thomas Aquinas (circa 1225–1274)
Sant' Eustorgio, Milan, Italy

St. Augustine (354–430)
Saint Pietro in Ciel D'Oro, Pavia, Italy

Francis Bacon (1561–1626)
Church of St. Michael, St. Albans, United Kingdom

Henri Bergson (1859–1941)
Cimetiere de Garches, Hauts de Seine, France

George Berkeley (1685–1753)
Christ Church Cathedral, Oxford, England

Nicolaus Copernicus (1473–1543)

Saint John's Cathedral, Frombork, Poland

René Descartes (1596–1650)

The Pantheon, Paris, France

John Dewey (1859–1952)

Dewey Memorial, Burlington, Vermont

Denis Diderot (1713–1784)

Church of Saint–Roch, Paris, France

Johann Gottlieb Fichte (1762–1814)

Dorotheenstäd and Friedrichswerder Cemetery, Berlin, Germany

Georg Hegel (1770–1831)

Dorotheenstäd and Friedrichswerder Cemetery, Berlin, Germany

Martin Heidegger (1889–1976)

Messkirch Town Cemetery, Messkirch, Baden–Wurttemberg, Germany

Thomas Hobbes (1588–1679)

Ault Hucknall Cemetery, Ault Hucknall, England

David Hume (1711–1776)

Old Calton Burial Ground, Edinburgh, Scotland

William James (1842–1910)

Cambridge Cemetery, Cambridge, Massachusetts

Immanuel Kant (1724–1804)

Kaliningrad Cemetery, Kaliningrad, Russia

Søren Kierkegaard (1813–1855)
Assistens Cemetery, Copenhagen, Denmark

Gottfried Wilhelm Leibniz (1646–1716)
Die Neustaedter Hof und Stadtkirche St. Johannis, Hanover, Germany

John Locke (1632–1704)
Christ Church Cathedral, Oxford, England

Niccolò Machiavelli (1469–1527)
Santa Croce Church, Florence, Italy

Karl Marx (1818–1883)
Highgate Cemetery (East), Highgate, London, England

John Stewart Mill (1806–1873)
Cimetiere de St. Véran, Avignon, France

Friedrich Nietzsche (1844–1900)
Röcken Churchyard, Rocken, Germany

Jean-Jacques Rousseau (1712–1778)
The Pantheon, Paris, France

Bertrand Russell (1872–1970)
Trinity College Chapel, Cambridge, England

Jean–Paul Sartre (1905–1980)
Cimitière Montparnasse, Paris, France

Arthur Schopenhauer (1788–1860)
Hauptfreidhof, Frankfurt–on–Main, Germany

Voltaire (1694–1778)

The Pantheon (empty sarcophagus), Paris, France

Ludwig Wittgenstein (1889–1951)

St. Giles Church yard, Cambridge, England

WHAT THEY SAID ABOUT DEATH

"I don't believe in an afterlife, so I don't have to spend my whole life fearing hell, or fearing heaven even more. For whatever the tortures of hell, I think the boredom of heaven would be even worse."

—Isaac Asimov

"Be of good cheer about death, and know this of a truth, that no evil can happen to a good man, either in life or after death."

—Socrates

"Only those are fit to live who do not fear to die; and none are fit to die who have shrunk from the joy of life and the duty of life. Both life and death are parts of the same Great Adventure."

—Theodore Roosevelt

"I do not believe that any man fears to be dead, but only the stroke of death."

—Francis Bacon

"There are but three events in a man's life: birth, life and death. He is conscious of being born, he dies in pain, and he forgets to live."

—Jean de La Bruyere

"The primary question about life after death is not whether it is a fact, but even if it is, what problems that really solves."

—Ludwig Wittgenstein

"Every man's life ends the same way. It is only the details of how he lived and how he died that distinguish one man from another."

—Ernest Hemingway

"Maybe this world is another planet's hell."

—Aldous Huxley

"I'm not afraid to die. I just don't want to be there when it happens."

—Woody Allen

"Do not take life too seriously. You will never get out of it alive."

—Elbert Hubbard

"That's all folks."

—Epitaph on the tombstone of Mel Blanc, who supplied the voices of Bugs Bunny, Porky Pig, and Daffy Duck

MODERN PHILOSOPHY

When they say "Size doesn't matter,"
they will probably lie about other things too.

When the going gets tough,
it's good to have four wheel drive.

No matter how bad things seem to be,
they can always get worse.

An ounce of prevention
usually comes in suppository form.

The hardest problems we face in life
seem trivial compared to an agonizing death.

Putting other people down
helps me forget my own private hell.

If you had just three wishes
you could always use one of the wishes
to wish for more wishes.

If all the peoples of the world
could live together in harmony,
it would probably be bad for the economy.

I don't remember being born,
so I probably won't remember dying.

People who ask for advice
never really want it.

Agnostics should just make up their minds already.

Money makes the world go around,
but the sun's gravity also has a lot to do with it.

A match made in heaven
can be hell on earth.

When you're on the road to self–discovery,
don't get off at the wrong exit.

If you live each day like it is your last,
the credit card company will still
want their money at the end of the month.

What goes up
might come down and hit you in the head.

What goes around
can sometimes be avoided
if you wash your hands frequently.

Women want to talk about problems,
men want to fix them,
and dogs don't give a damn.

No matter how much you've eaten,
there is always room for Jell–O.

No one has ever survived a plane crash
because his seat was in the upright position
and his tray table was locked.

Good fences make good neighbors,
but nymphomaniac swimsuit models make the best.

The more things change, the more they cost.

The true test of friendship
is whether someone will help you move a dead body.

Honesty is the best policy
unless you're a mass murderer on the witness stand.

It's better to wait five minutes for the pizza to cool down
than burn the roof of your mouth.

I was sad because I had no shoes
until I went to the bowling alley
and saw the shoes they rent.

The only law no one breaks
is the law of gravity.

If all the people in the world were to lay down end to end,
they'd be much more comfortable.

You can kiss the bride after the wedding,
but not three years after the wedding.

There are no atheists
when there's turbulence at 30,000 feet.

No matter how hot and steamy a relationship is at first,
the inflatable doll is bound to spring a leak.

It's better to have loved and lost
than to be nagged about buying a
damn anniversary gift every year.

It takes more than a minute to make Minute Rice.

The journey of a thousand miles
begins with one phone call to a travel agent.

If at first you don't succeed,
go to night school.

The light at the end of the tunnel
is another train heading straight for you.

If eyes are the windows to the soul,
then eyelids are the Venetian blinds.

If you ever find yourself with
a group of teenagers in the woods
being stalked by a psycho killer wearing a hockey mask,
don't go off by yourself with a flashlight to get help.

Those who cannot remember the past
are condemned to nursing homes.

Bad people sometimes do good things,
and good people sometimes do bad things,
but my brother–in–law never seems to do anything.

When you wish upon a star
you will soon hear from Disney's trademark attorneys.

If at first you don't succeed,
add "dot.com" to the company name.

It is easier to smile while the world is crashing down around you
if you've kept your resume up to date.

Time heals all wounds
but not necessarily before you bleed to death.

THINKERS AND STINKERS

NASTY NIETZSCHE

- Born October 15, 1844, in the small German town of Röcken bei Lützen, Friedrich Wilhelm Nietzsche was named after Prussian King Friedrich Wilhelm IV, who was born on the exact same day forty-nine years earlier and who had been responsible for Nietzsche's father's appointment as Röcken's town minister.

- Nietzsche's family called him "Fritz."

- Nietzsche grew up as the only male in a house of five females: his mother, his grandmother, his two aunts, and his younger sister.

- Nietzsche became close friends with composer Richard Wagner, thirty-one years his senior, and seen by many as a replacement for Nietzsche's father, who died when Nietzsche was four years old.

- As a teenager, Nietzsche began composing piano, choral, and orchestral music.

- At the age of twenty-one, Nietzsche accidentally discovered a copy of Arthur Schopenhauer's *The World as Will and Representation* in a local bookstore. The book changed his life.

- While serving in the military in an equestrian field artillery regiment, Nietzsche lived at home with his mother.

- Nietzsche began teaching as a member of the classical philology faculty at the University of Basel at the age of twenty-four.

- While serving as a hospital attendant during the Franco–Prussian War (1870–71), Nietzsche contracted diphtheria and dysentery. Subsequently, he endured health problems for the rest of his life.

- At the age of thirty-two, Nietzsche proposed marriage to a Dutch piano student living in Geneva named Mathilde Trampedach. She turned him down.

- The publication of Nietzsche's book *Human, All Too Human* in 1878 marked the end of his friendship with composer Richard Wagner, who Nietzsche disparaged in his thinly–disguised characterization of "the artist."

- From 1880 until 1889, Nietzsche led a nomadic existence as a man without a country (giving up his German citizenship and failing to acquire Swiss citizenship).

- At the age of thirty-seven, Nietzsche proposed marriage to a twenty-one-year-old Russian philosophy student in Zurich named Lou Salomé, who turned him down. Salomé later worked with Sigmund Freud and wrote her psychological insights regarding her relationship with Nietzsche.

- On January 3, 1889, while in Turin, Italy, Nietzsche witnessed a horse being whipped by a coachman at the Piazza Carlo Alberto. Nietzsche threw his arms around the horse's neck and collapsed with a nervous breakdown, never regaining his sanity.

- No one knows the exact cause of Nietzsche's breakdown. Doctors in Basel and Jena diagnosed Nietzsche with a syphilitic infection, which the philosopher could have contracted as a student or while serving as a hospital attendant during the Franco–Prussian War. Nietzsche had used the drug chloral hydrate as a sedative, which some say shattered his fragile nervous system. Others suggest that Nietzsche's collapse was the result of a brain disease he inherited from his father. Still others insist that a mental illness gradually drove him insane.

- After his breakdown, Nietzsche spent a year in a sanatorium in Jena, and was cared for by his mother at her home for the next seven years until her death, when his sister Elisabeth took responsibility for his welfare—allowing visitors to observe the debilitated philosopher.

- Before assuming responsibility for Nietzsche's care, his sister Elisabeth worked in Paraguay with her husband Bernhard Förster to establish an Aryan, anti-Semitic German colony called Nueva Germania ("New Germany").

Nietzsche Condensed ➡️⬅️

Urging people to re-evaluate and reconstruct their value systems, Nietzsche believed that each individual should master self–control over his animal instincts and rechannel those passions through creativity, fully embracing life to the fullest for the benefit of all mankind—possibly explaining why he went insane.

WHAT NIETZSCHE SAID

"One must have a good memory to be able to keep the promises one makes."

"The man of knowledge must be able not only to love his enemies but also to hate his friends."

"Nothing on earth consumes a man more quickly than the passion of resentment."

"You shall become the person you are."

"God is dead! God stays dead! And we killed him."

"Morality is herd instinct in the individual."

"The Christian resolution to find the world ugly and bad has made the world ugly and bad."

"The most perfidious way of harming a cause consists of defending it deliberately with faulty arguments."

"What is the sign of liberation? No longer being ashamed in front of oneself."

"The secret for harvesting from existence the greatest fruitfulness and greatest enjoyment is—to live dangerously."

"The advantage of a bad memory is that one enjoys several times the same good things for the first time."

"We are always in our own company."

"Plato is boring."

"What does not destroy me, makes me stronger."

"Without music, life would be an error."

"It is my ambition to say in ten sentences what everyone else says in a whole book—what everyone else does *not* say in a whole book."

"Some are born posthumously."

"Love is a state in which a man sees things most decidedly as they are *not*."

"God created woman. And boredom did indeed cease from that moment—but many other things ceased as well! Woman was God's *second* mistake."

"A casual stroll through the lunatic asylum shows that faith does not prove anything."

"Faith means not wanting to know what is true."

"No one is such a liar as the indignant man."

"In revenge and in love woman is more barbarous than man."

"The thought of suicide is a great consolation: by means of it one gets successfully through many a bad night."

"Blessed are the forgetful: for they get the better even of their blunders."

"Is not life a hundred times too short for us to bore ourselves?"

"One does not know—cannot know—the best that is in one."

"He who fights with monsters should see to it that in the process he himself does not become a monster. And when you gaze long into an abyss, the abyss also gazes into you."

"Distrust all in whom the impulse to punish is powerful."

"I should only believe in a God that would know how to dance."

Nietzsche and the Nazis

During the 1930s, the Nazis and Italian Fascists espoused facets of Nietzsche's ideas, due in part to his racist sister Elisabeth Förster's appeals to Adolf Hitler and Benito Mussolini. The Nazi propaganda machine conveniently selected and juxtaposed passages taken out of context from Nietzsche's writings and misrepresented the concept of Nietzsche's *Übermensch* (or Overman) to promote "Aryan" superiority as the master race, justify brutality, and validate Germany's war to dominate Europe. Like Nietzsche, Hitler idolized the music of Richard Wagner. The Nazi propaganda machine conveniently neglected quotes from Nietzsche that undermined its position. Wrote Nietzsche: "Wherever Germany extends her sway, she ruins culture" and "The Germans are like women, you can scarcely ever fathom their depths—they haven't any."

IDEAS ABOUT IDEAS

Where do our ideas come from? Does God plant them in our heads? Do we originate them completely on our own? Or do we copy them word for word from the encyclopedia? Are we born with a limited supply of ideas that slowly trickle out of our brains like ketchup from a bottle? Or do we have an endless supply of ketchup? If you have no idea, consider these ideas:

The Sophists (fifth century BCE)

Knowledge is subjective and depends upon each individual. To you, the glass is half full. To me, the glass needs to be run through the dishwasher.

Socrates (469–399 BCE)

Knowledge is the key to solving problems, but we can establish definitive principles only by separating fact from opinion. To do this, we use inductive and deductive logic. And sometimes a polygraph test and sodium pentothal.

Heraclitus (circa 535–circa 475 BCE)

Reason, a spark of the divine in man, is the source of knowledge, but most men allow passion to guide their lives. Of course, that should come as no surprise to the ladies.

Democritus (460–370 BCE)

Knowledge begins when we rise above sense perception. But please remain in your seats until the pilot has turned off the seatbelt sign.

Plato (circa 427–circa 347 BCE)

The soul, created in the realm of ideas and infused with knowledge, is implanted in man at birth. Man spends his life striving to remember all the knowledge ingrained in his soul. Not to mention all those SAT vocabulary words.

Aristotle (384–322 BCE)

Knowledge requires knowing what causes things, which can be acquired through the science of deductive logic, based on the pattern of "syllogism," moving from a general principle to a more specific principal, such as:

All men are pigs.
Socrates is a man.
Therefore Socrates is a pig.

Epicurus (circa 342–270 BCE)

We acquire knowledge through our senses by interpreting our perceptions correctly. That's why you're more likely to get laid if you're wearing beer goggles.

The Stoics (circa third century BCE)

Man is born without any ideas. The mind organizes our sense perceptions into ideas, building a vast warehouse of knowledge. Or in some cases, a tiny outhouse.

St. Augustine (354–430)

Man gets his ideas about nature through experience and logical reasoning, but receives his ideas about the spiritual realm through faith, revelation from God, or the Psychic Hotline.

Thomas Aquinas (circa 1225–1274)

The mind transforms perceptions received from sensations into knowledge, but the mind also has intuitive knowledge based on divine revelation. But absolutely no knowledge of any illegal activities.

Francis Bacon (1561–1626)

If man is to secure knowledge from observation, experiment, and understanding, he must clear his mind of prejudices and erroneous views, carefully collect all significant data, and strive to draw conclusions objectively. If the glove don't fit, you must acquit.

Galileo Galilei (1564–1642)

All knowledge comes from observation, experimentation, understanding, and the occasional lucky guess.

René Descartes (1596–1650)

Truth must be established on a foundation of indisputable premises that are clear and distinct, and upon these fundamental premises, knowledge can then be built one step at a time through careful reasoning. No wonder the line is so long at the post office.

Benedict Spinoza (1632–1677)

There are three kinds of knowledge: inadequate ideas (sense perceptions interpreted incorrectly), rational knowledge (ideas acquired by reasoning through previously known information), and intuitive knowledge (indisputable truth). And this qualifies as a really weird idea.

John Locke (1632–1704)

Simple ideas come through sense perceptions, and the mind organizes these simple ideas into complex ideas. "Hmmm, this Twinkie tastes really good. I bet it would taste even better deep fried."

Gottfried Wilhelm Leibniz (1646–1716)

Man is composed of monads, which cannot be affected or influenced by any outside force, and each monad contains all of the ideas in the universe. Or at least how to make toast.

George Berkeley (1685–1753)

We receive our ideas from God. Usually by three–day ground delivery.

David Hume (1711–1776)

The mind is a sequence of ideas, and we have no way to know for certain if we get these ideas from our sense perceptions of a truly existent material world or directly from God. Either way, I'm not paying seven dollars for a beer.

Immanuel Kant (1724–1804)

The mind receives impressions of the environment through the senses and then shapes these impressions into ideas. Now please pass the salt.

Johann Gottlieb Fichte (1762–1814)

The universal ego creates the ideas in our minds. Free of charge.

Georg Wilhelm Friedrich Hegel (1770–1831)

The mind develops a thesis, then an antithesis, then unifies these opposites into a synthesis, which becomes the thesis for yet more complex syntheses—until you get a throbbing migraine.

Johann Friedrich Herbart (1776–1841)

The thought process is the organization and integration of "reals." In other words, the mind is one massive accounting office where the bookkeeping never gets done.

John Stuart Mill (1806–1873)

Through experience, the individual collects data, from which he studiously draws conclusions, carefully infers generalizations, and impulsively jumps to ridiculous assumptions.

William James (1842–1910)

Ideas are a result of the thinking process. Or else they're planted in your mind by extraterrestrial beings hellbent on world domination.

John Dewey (1859–1952)

Man thinks only when he has a problem to solve. For each problem, he takes the same basic steps. He defines the problem, collects pertinent data, uses the data as a basis for arriving at a possible solution, mentally tests the proposed solution to seek any flaws with the plan, executes the plan, and records the results for future thought. Or he wisely decides to ignore the problem and hope it goes away by itself.

THE SHIRLEY PARTRIDGE PHILOSOPHY

In the hit 1970s television sitcom *The Partridge Family,* a recently widowed mother named Shirley Partridge becomes a permanent member of her children's rock band, driving the group to gigs aboard a school bus repainted in the colorful geometric style of Piet Mondrian, just like the psychedelic bus in Tom Wolfe's book *The Electric Kool–Aid Acid Test,* the Beatles' movie *Magical Mystery Tour,* and the Who's song "Magic Bus." Along the way, Shirley, played by actress and singer Shirley Jones, philosophically dished out hip motherly advice, echoing the thoughts of the world's greatest thinkers.

"Man is a prisoner who has no right to open the door of his prison and run away."

—Plato

"I can't imagine what it's like to be a convict, but I think in some real way, we're all prisoners."

—Shirley Partridge

"Nonviolence is the first article of my faith. It is also the last article of my creed."

—Mahatma Gandhi

"Maybe threats are your solution to a problem, but they're not mine. I haven't decided what I'm going to do yet, but I will not allow you to intimidate my family. Is that clear?"

—Shirley Partridge

"A man of genius makes no mistakes. His errors are volitional and are the portals of discovery."

—James Joyce

"You can't give up just because you've made mistakes. You can do anything you want to do as long as you're willing to keep trying and not afraid of making more mistakes. Almost everything we know is learned by trial and error."

—Shirley Partridge

"If you are lucky enough to live in Paris as a young man, then wherever you go for the rest of your life, it stays with you, for Paris is a moveable feast."

—Ernest Hemingway

"[Paris is] kind of a Disneyland for grown-ups."

—Shirley Partridge

"Laws are like cobwebs, which may catch small flies, but let wasps and hornets break through."

—Jonathan Swift

"There's no sense in calling the police or running away. That never solves anything."

—Shirley Partridge

"It's a kind of spiritual snobbery that makes people think they can be happy without money."

—Albert Camus

"There's nothing wrong with money, if you work for it. It's a symbol for your labor so you can respect it and appreciate it. But if it's given to you, it isn't the same. It isn't really yours."

—Shirley Partridge

"Unthread the rude eye of rebellion,
And welcome home again discarded faith."

—William Shakespeare

"If you force a child to stay at home, it's only going to make him want to run away more."

—Shirley Partridge

"If anything is sacred, the human body is sacred."

—Walt Whitman

"The human body is beautiful. There's nothing wrong with it . . . but it doesn't belong on a garage."

—Shirley Partridge

"Justice is my being allowed to do whatever I like. Injustice is whatever prevents my doing so."

—Samuel Johnson

"It's never too late for justice."

—Shirley Partridge

"If youth is a defect, it is one that we outgrow too soon."

—Robert Lowell

"It may sound corny, but some people think that being a kid is the best time of your life. Most kids never realize that."

—Shirley Partridge

"It is not the strength but the duration of great sentiments that makes great men."

—Friedrich Nietzsche

"You can't put a price on sentiment."

—Shirley Partridge

"Those who cannot remember the past are condemned to repeat it."

—George Santayana

"Saying you're sorry doesn't always erase the thing you do."

—Shirley Partridge

"A truth that's told with bad intent
Beats all the lies you can invent."

—William Blake

"Sometimes the truth can be misused. The important thing is that you care about people."

—Shirley Partridge

"We are apt to shut our eyes against a painful truth, and listen to the song of that siren till she transforms us into beasts."

—Patrick Henry

"You shouldn't be afraid to tell me the truth, even if it does hurt a little."

—Shirley Partridge

"If you're not part of the solution, you're part of the problem."

—H. Rap Brown

"Instead of sitting here complaining about the way things are, why don't you do something about it?"

—Shirley Partridge

"Gossip is mischievous, light and easy to raise, but grievous to bear and hard to dismiss."

—Hesiod

"You can't believe rumors."

—Shirley Partridge

"Pains of love be sweeter far
Than all other pleasures are."

—John Dryden

"As you get older, you'll find out that most of the time, love doesn't work out the way you want it to, and it does hurt."

—Shirley Partridge

"If one advances confidently in the direction of his dreams, and endeavors to live the life which he has imagined, he will meet with a success unexpected in common hours."

—Henry David Thoreau

"Most things in life that people want aren't just handed to them. If you really want something, you have to keep trying."

—Shirley Partridge

"Knowledge is power."

—Francis Bacon

"You won't learn anything unless you do your own homework."

—Shirley Partridge

"It is a consolation to the wretched to have companions in misery."

—Publilius Syrus

"Too bad it took an energy crisis for us to realize how much fun it is just to sit around together."

—Shirley Partridge

" 'Tis better to have loved and lost
Than never to have loved at all."

—Alfred, Lord Tennyson

"Sometime or another, everyone has to face losing. I know it's hard, but it isn't the end of the world. I mean, after all, if people didn't lose sometime, I guess winning wouldn't mean very much."

—Shirley Partridge

"I see the cure is not worth the pain."

—Plutarch

"Sometimes when you try not to hurt someone, you end up hurting yourself more."

—Shirley Partridge

———————————— 🚺 ————————————

"We find it as difficult to forgive a person for displaying his feeling in all its nakedness as we do to forgive a man for being penniless."

—Honoré de Balzac

"You can forgive anyone who acts out of love."

—Shirley Partridge

THINKERS AND STINKERS

CUCKOO FOR KIERKEGAARD

- In grammar school, Danish philosopher Søren Kierkegaard (1813–1855) was nicknamed "the Fork," for his ability to rip his antagonists apart with his dialectical skills.

- Kierkegaard seldom left his hometown of Copenhagen. He left his home country of Denmark only five times—four times to travel to Berlin and once to travel to Sweden.

- As an adult, Kierkegaard briefly taught Latin at the grammar school he had attended as a child.

- In his essay "From the Papers of One Still Living Published Against His Will," Kierkegaard reviews Hans Christian Andersen's novel *Only A Fiddler,* which he criticizes for lacking a "life view." In his autobiography, *The Fairy Tale of My Life,* Andersen wrote that he and Kierkegaard were probably the only two people who had read "From the Papers of One Still Living." In his fairy tale "Galoshes of Fortune," Andersen caricatures Kierkegaard as a parrot, and in his play "A Comedy in the Open Air: Vaudeville in One Act Based on the Old Comedy An Actor Against His Will," Andersen caricatures Kierkegaard as a hairdresser.

- Kierkegaard also wrote under several different pseudonyms, including Johannes Climacus and Johannes de Silentio, and sometimes wrote articles satirizing his own books under a different name.

- Kierkegaard's father believed that all seven of his children would die before reaching the age of thirty-three (the age at which Jesus was crucified). Only Søren and his brother Peter lived beyond the age of thirty-three.

- In 1840, Kierkegaard became engaged to seventeen–year–old Regine Olsen, but broke off the engagement the following year. Soon after, Regine married Kierkegaard's rival. Some scholars say Kierkegaard broke off his engagement to Regine Olsen to intentionally sublimate his sexual energy into his work.

- In 1845, Denmark's satirical paper *The Corsair* published a critique of Kierkegaard's book *Stages of Life's Way*. In response, Kierkegaard wrote *Dialectical Result of a Literary Police Action,* attacking *The Corsair* and asking to be lampooned. *The Corsair* obliged, lambasting Kierkegaard for several months and caricaturing him mercilessly.

Kierkegaard Condensed ➡️⬅️

Considered one of the founders of Existentialism, Kierkegaard insisted that religious faith is irrational and requires acceptance of the absurd. Kierkegaard willingly made this leap of faith, without the aid of a swift kick in the ass from the church.

WHAT KIERKEGAARD SAID

"Life can only be understood backwards; but it must be lived forwards."

"Be that self which one truly is."

"If I were to wish for anything, I should not wish for wealth and power, but for the passionate sense of potential—for the eye which, ever young and ardent, sees the possible. Pleasure disappoints; possibility never."

"I divide my time as follows: half the time I sleep, the other half I dream. I never dream when I sleep, for that would be a pity, for sleeping is the highest accomplishment of genius."

"What is a poet? An unhappy person who conceals profound anguish in his heart but whose lips are so formed that as sighs and cries pass over them they sound like beautiful music."

"No time of life is so beautiful as the early days of love, when with every meeting, every glance, one fetches something new home to rejoice over."

"Genius never desires what does not exist."

"In addition to my other numerous acquaintances, I have one more intimate confidant . . . . My depression is the most faithful mistress I have known—no wonder, then, that I return the love."

"There is nothing with which every man is so afraid as getting to know how enormously much he is capable of doing and becoming."

"The way to love anything is to realize it might be lost."

"During the first period of a man's life the greatest danger is not to take the risk. When once the risk has really been taken, then the greatest danger is to risk too much."

WHAT THEY SAID ABOUT IDEAS

"The test of a first–rate intelligence is the ability to hold two opposed ideas in the mind at the same time, and still retain the ability to function."

—F. Scott Fitzgerald

"Anyone who has begun to think places some portion of the world in jeopardy."

—John Dewey

"There is one thing stronger than all the armies in the world, and that is an idea who time has come."

—Victor Hugo

"Change your thoughts and you change your world."

—Norman Vincent Peale

"Millions say the apple fell, but Newton was the one to ask why."

—Bernard M. Baruch

"The mind is its own place, and in itself can make a heaven of Hell, a hell of Heaven."

—John Milton

"The best ideas are common property."

—Lucius Annaeus Seneca

"We are prisoners of ideas."

—Ralph Waldo Emerson

"Nature has planted in our minds an insatiable longing to see the truth."

—Marcus Tullius Cicero

"We are healthy only to the extent that our ideas are humane."

—Kurt Vonnegut

"The best way to have a good idea is to have lots of ideas."

—Linus Pauling

"Any man who afflicts the human race with ideas must be prepared to see them misunderstood."

—H. L. Mencken

"All human knowledge thus begins with intuitions, proceeds thence to concepts, and ends with ideas."

—Immanuel Kant

"I can't understand why people are frightened of new ideas. I'm frightened of the old ones."

—John Cage

"Ideas are like rabbits. You get a couple and learn how to handle them, and pretty soon you have a dozen."

—John Steinbeck

"If you have an apple and I have an apple and we exchange these apples, then you and I will still each have one apple. But if you have an idea and I have an idea and we exchange these ideas, then each of us will have two ideas."

—George Bernard Shaw

SMART BABES: NINE FEMALE PHILOSOPHERS

You don't hear much about female philosophers, because hey, it's a sexist world out there, but here are some heady hotties who could give Descartes, Spinoza, and Hegel something to think about.

Hipparchia the Cynic (circa fourth century)

A Greek philosopher, Hipparchia embraced the Cynic belief in shamelessness so ardently that she purportedly consummated her marriage to fellow philosopher Crates by engaging in sex on a public porch.

Elisabeth of Bohemia (circa 1617–1680)

For seven years, the German Elisabeth corresponded with her teacher René Descartes about philosophy and critically asked him how the mind and body—if they are separate entities as Descartes insisted—interact. Stumped, Descartes never replied.

Anne Finch Conway (1631–1679)

Her sole book, *The Principles of the Most Ancient and Modern Philosophy*, published in English after her death, critiqued the philosophy of Hobbes, Descartes, and Spinoza, attempted to reconcile why a benevolent God permits evil and suffering, and influenced Gottfried Wilhelm Leibniz.

Mary Astell (1666–1731)

An English philosopher, Astell advocated equal educational opportunities for women and wrote several books, including *A Serious Proposal to the Ladies, Parts I and II: Wherein a Method is Offer'd for the Improvement of their Minds*.

Mary Wollstonecraft (1759–1797)

In her 1792 book *A Vindication of the Rights of Woman*, Mary Wollstonecraft argues that boys and girls should be educated equally, in response to Rousseau's book *Émile*, which argues that boys should be given a better education than girls. Wollstonecraft was the mother of Mary Shelley, who later wrote the novel *Frankenstein*, which integrates many ideas from *A Vindication of the Rights of Woman*.

Mary Whiton Calkins (1863–1930)

An American philosopher and psychologist who wrote the book *The Persistent Problems of Philosophy,* Calkins argued that the universe is a conscious, intellectual, personal being. Although Harvard University repeatedly refused to grant her a Ph.D., despite the protests of Harvard alumni, Calkins became the first female president of the American Psychological Association.

Ayn Rand (1905–1982)

A Russian–born Jewish–American author, Rand developed the philosophy of Objectivism and wrote several renowned novels, including *We the Living, Anthem, The Fountainhead*, and *Atlas Shrugged*, stressing individualism and rational self–interest. Rand, who worked in Hollywood as a screenwriter, married actor Frank O'Connor, whom she met on the set of the 1927 Cecil B. DeMille movie *The King of Kings* by tripping him.

Hannah Arendt (1906–1975)

A Jewish–German political theorist, Arent despised being called a philosopher because she felt philosophy concerns the singular man rather than the whole of mankind. Romantically involved with German philosopher Martin Heidegger, who sympathized with the Nazis, Arent fled Nazi Germany in 1933, first to France, then to the United States. In 1959, she became the first woman appointed to a full professorship at Princeton University.

Simone de Beauvoir (1908–1986)

A French philosopher best know for her 1949 treatise *The Second Sex*, de Beauvoir met French existentialist Jean–Paul Sartre while she was studying philosophy at the Sorbonne, where she was nicknamed *Castor* (French for "beaver")—a pun based on the resemblance of her surname to the English word *beaver*. In 1943, de Beauvoir published her novel *L'Invitée (She Came to Stay)*, based on her lesbian relationship with her student Olga Kosakiewicz and their *ménage a trois* with Sartre.

ACKNOWLEDGMENTS

At Running Press, I am grateful to my editor Jennifer Kasius for her passion, enthusiasm, and excitement for this book. I am also deeply indebted to my publisher Jon Anderson, researcher Debbie Green, expert copyeditor Nancy Armstrong, designer Josh McDonnell, and cover illustrator Blake Loosli.

A very special thanks to my agent Stephanie Tade for her wonderful philosophy toward life, my pal Mike Reiss, and the witty Elaine White.

Above all, all my love to Debbie, Ashley, and Julia.

BIBLIOGRAPHY

- *Basic Teachings of the Great Philosophers* by S. E. Frost Jr. (New York: Doubleday, 1962).

- *Being and Time* by Martin Heidegger, translated by John MacQuarrie and Edward Robinson (London, SCM Press,1962).

- *The Best, the Worst and Most Unusual* by B. Felton and M. Fowler (New York: Galahad, 1994).

- *Candide, or Optimism* by Voltaire, translated by Peter Constantine (New York: Modern Library, 2005)

- *Classics of Western Philosophy, Fifth Edition,* edited by Steven M. Cahn (Indianapolis: Hackett Publishing, 1999).

- *Cogito, Ergo Sum: The Life of René Descartes* by Richard Watson (Boston: David R. Godine, 2002).

- *The Communist* Manifesto by Karl Marx and Friedrich Engels, edited by Samuel H. Beer (Northbrook, Illinois: AHM Publishing, 1955).

- *Critique of Pure Reason* by Immanuel Kant, translated by J.M.D. Meiklejohn (London: Dent, 1946).

- *A Dictionary of Philosophy, Revised Second Edition* by Antony Flew (New York: St. Martin's Press, 1979).

- *An Essay Concerning Human Understanding* by John Locke (London: Dent, 1965).

- *Familiar Quotations, Fifteenth Edition* by John Bartlett (Boston: Little, Brown, 1980).

- *Five Great Dialogues* by Plato (Roslyn, New York: Walter J. Black, 1942)

- *Introduction of Modern Existentialism* by Ernst Breisach (New York: Grove Press, 1962).

- *Leviathan* by Thomas Hobbes (London: Dutton, 1975)

- *Meditations on First Philosophy* by René Descartes (Cambridge, England: Cambridge University Press, 1986).

- *The Myth of Sisyphus and Other Essays* by Albert Camus, translated by Justin O'Brien (New York: Vintage Books, 1991).

- *Nicomachean Ethics* by Aristotle (Oxford: Oxford University Press, 2002).

- *No Exit: And Three Other Plays* by Jean-Paul Sartre (New York: Vintage, 1955)

- *The Oxford Dictionary of Modern Quotations* by Tony Augarde (Oxford, England: Oxford University Press, 1991).

- *The Oxford Dictionary of Quotations, Third Edition* (Oxford, England: Oxford University Press, 1979).

- *Peter's Quotations: Ideas for Our Time* by Dr. Laurence J. Peter (New York: Bantam, 1977).

- *Philosophy: An Introduction to the Art of Wondering* by James L. Christian (Fort Worth: Harcourt Brace College Publishers, 1994)

- *Philosophy, 100 Essential Thinkers* by Philip Stokes (New York: Enchanted Lion, 2003)

- *Philosophy: The Basics* by Nigel Warburton (New York: Routledge, 2004).

- *The Prince* by Niccolò Machiavelli, translated by Peter Bondanella and Mark Musa (Oxford, England: Oxford University Press, 1979).

- *The Problems of Philosophy* by Bertrand Russell (New York: Oxford University Press, 1997).

- *Reader's Digest Book of Facts* (Pleasantville, New York: Reader's Digest, 1987).

- *Ripley's Believe It or Not! Encyclopedia of the Bizarre* by Julie Mooney and the editors of Ripley's Believe It or Not (New York: Black Dog & Leventhal, 2002).

- *The Social Contract and the First and Second Discourses* by Jean-Jacques Rousseau; edited by Susan Dunn (New Haven, Connecticut: Yale University Press, 2002).

- *Story of Philosophy: The Lives and Opinions of the World's Greatest Philosophers* by Will Durant (New York: Pocket Books, 1991).

- *The Story of Philosophy* by Bryan Magee (New York: DK Publishing, 2001).

- *A Treatise of Human Nature* by David Hume, edited by David Fate Norton and Mary J. Norton (Oxford, England: Oxford University Press, 2000)

- *Thus Spake Zarathurstra* by Friedrich Nietzsche, translated by Thomas Common (Mineola, New York: Dover Publications, 1999).

- *Twenty Questions: An Introduction to Philosophy, sixth edition* by G. Lee Bowie, Meredith W. Michaels, Robert C. Solomon (Belmont, California: Wadsworth Publishing, 2006).

- *Utilitarianism* by John Stuart Mill (Indianapolis: Bobbs–Merrill, 1957).

- *Where Are They Buried? How Did They Die? Fitting Ends and Final Resting Places of the Famous, Infamous, and Noteworthy* by Tod Benoit (New York: Black Dog and Leventhal, 2003).

- *World Religions: From Ancient History to the Present*, edited by Geoffrey Parrinder (New York: Facts on File, 1985).

- *World Scripture: A Comparative Anthology of Sacred Texts,* edited by Andrew Wilson (St. Paul, Minnesota: Paragon House, 1995).

INDEX

ABOUT THE AUTHOR

Joey Green—author of *Polish Your Furniture with Panty Hose, Paint Your House with Powdered Milk, Wash Your Hair with Whipped Cream*, and *Clean Your Clothes with Cheez Wiz*—got Jay Leno to shave with Jif Peanut Butter on *The Tonight Show*, Rosie O'Donnell to mousse her hair with Jell-O on *The Rosie O'Donnell Show*, and had Katie Couric drop her diamond engagement ring in a glass of Efferdent on *Today*. He has been seen polishing furniture with SPAM on *NBC Dateline*, cleaning a toilet with Coca-Cola in the *New York Times*, and washing his hair with Reddi-wip in *People*.

Green, a former contributing editor to *National Lampoon* and a former advertising copywriter at J. Walter Thompson, is the author of forty books, including *Marx & Lennon: The Parallel Sayings, Weird Christmas,* and *The Zen of Oz: Ten Spiritual Lessons from Over the Rainbow*. A native of Miami, Florida, and a graduate of Cornell University, he wrote television commercials for Burger King and Walt Disney World and won a Clio Award for a print ad he created for Eastman Kodak. He backpacked around the world for two years on his honeymoon and lives in Los Angeles with his wife, Debbie, and their two daughters, Ashley and Julia.

For more offbeat uses for brand-name products,
visit Joey Green on the Internet at: www.wackyuses.com